An Intentional Marriage

Making your Wedding Day Vows

an Everyday Reality

By Kristen and Chad Cottingham

ISBN: 9798444480144

We dedicate this book to our mothers, Judy (Dense')
Niedrach and Marian Cottingham–Schleisman, who are
beautiful examples of living out their wedding day vows
"until death do us apart."

We are truly grateful for their love and support.

*"Her children stand and bless her... There are many
virtuous and capable women in the world, but you
surpass them all." (Proverbs 31: 28-29)*

Table of Contents

Introduction

Weddings have become a billion dollar a year industry that continues to boom. There doesn't seem to be a shortage of photographers, planners, bakers, or barns waiting to host the fairy tale wedding couples dream of. So much time and money are spent planning and preparing for this one day. Don't get me wrong, it is a special day that deserves careful thought and consideration to detail but it only lasts for one day. In contrast, consider how much time and money is spent on the marriage itself?

Many couples invest in some pre-marital counseling, but that's typically where it ends. If and when couples seek counsel or expertise is usually when things have gone south – when reality doesn't match their envisioned ideal. However, in most of life's worthwhile endeavors, whether it be our job, hobby, or passion there is usually some form of training, education, coaching, or even YouTube video we pursue to continue our development and advancement. The one area that many seem to detour from the pursuit of growth in is marriage. That was us. We sought knowledge and advice here and there but did little on a regular basis to grow and build our marriage.

After thirty years we can honestly say marriage is one of the hardest, most challenging things we've encountered. However, it is also the most rewarding, fulfilling and life-giving experience too. Yes, both extremes exist. We learned the hard way that great marriages don't happen without effort. No couple just drifts in the right direction. We have to make an intentional effort to keep growing and becoming better spouses. Along the way, we discovered the secret lies in the vows we made on our wedding day. They are the rudder that steers our ship and keeps it from running aground or worse yet, sinking. So, what if we spent our time and energy making our wedding vows an everyday reality?

I want to thank you for joining us on our journey. As Kristen will share, it has been a very bumpy ride for us. One that starts with two kids meeting in college, falling in love and then getting married quickly because of an unplanned pregnancy. It has been marked with financial struggles, heartbreaking loss, and poor marital decisions. It's a journey through depression and heartache, tears and fights, and is about two people who were just downright selfish. Our story speaks to God's grace and mercy that held us together when we couldn't even hold ourselves up.

And we wouldn't change one heartache, one fight - anything. Because it was through it all that God taught us how to love and forgive, how to give up our pride and control, and how to enjoy each other along the way. We don't have all of the answers but we hope you find hope and help, encouragement and inspiration and that you, too, will become intentional about making your wedding day vows and everyday reality.

May God bless your marriage,

Chad

I.

To Have and To Hold

Strengthening Friendship

A safe friendship is the foundation of a lasting and happy marriage.

1. The Beginning

A new beginning is like receiving a gift from a trusted friend who sits eagerly, watching in anticipation as we unwrap the surprise, encouraging us to open up and receive thrilling possibilities. Whether it is turning to the first page of a long-awaited book, starting another job, or entering a different season, a new beginning releases an excitement that swirls around our heart like a kite in the wind. Perhaps the most exhilarating beginning of all is a new relationship.

For a moment, think back to the very first time you laid eyes on your spouse. Maybe it was as recently as a year ago, or perhaps it's been more than thirty years. Can you recall the beginning of your life together? Is your first impression still

7

painted vividly on the canvas of your mind? Do you remember details like the exact date, the location, what you were wearing, and who you were with? Did your heart skip a beat as you locked eyes, your stomach fluttering with exhilaration, or did you dismiss their presence casually? Was this special moment one that caused you to catch your breath as your heart stirred at the potential of an exciting, new beginning?

Our story began Saturday, August 19, 1989. It was the day my parents dropped me off at Liberty University in Lynchburg, Virginia. I was seventeen, seven hundred miles from home, and knew only two other girls who I was supposed to be meeting for dinner that evening. I waited around in the commons area of the main building, but my friends were so late, I thought they weren't going to show. I could not waste another minute just sitting around with the anticipation of a new beginning popping like champagne bubbles in my body, so I decided to venture out in search of the action.

I pushed open the double doors of the main building and entered the courtyard area, feeling like a celebrity stepping out of a limousine. I believed the world was my stage and I was the star of the show. I quickly scanned the landscape—a vast sea of students all huddled in little groups. As I weaved my way through the crowd, I hoped my confident exterior would override the momentary internal uncertainty I felt as to where I was going. Then suddenly a red-haired guy jumped in front of me and blurted, "Hey, where are you from?" I answered tentatively, "I'm from Michigan." He turned and called out over his clique of friends, "Hey, Chad! This girl is from Michigan!"

Instantly, I was transported back into my imaginary movie scene. The spotlight shifted as the crowd parted like the Red Sea. Into the light stepped this good-looking guy wearing a burgundy polo shirt and stone-washed, French-rolled jeans (it was the '80s). His face radiated with a sparkling smile (literally sparkling because he had a silver bottom tooth), and I thought to myself, I think I'm going to like college. We chatted nervously for a few minutes, then I left to look for my girlfriends.

I eventually found them and convinced them to go back with me to look for this cute guy I just met. I really wanted to check him out again! He was still in the same spot, and when I saw him for the second time, my stomach felt like a tumble dryer with a tennis ball bouncing around inside. Over the next several days, we kept running into each other. I decided it must be fate and we began spending every spare minute together over the next few weeks. It did not take long for us to start dating officially.

I found out later that the reason Chad was even there that night was to scope out the new crop of freshman girls. He, being a sophomore, had convinced his buddy (who jumped out at me) to arrive a few days early so they could get first dibs on the new girls. Now, when we tell this part of our story I still tease him, "Are you sure that was such a good idea?"

Another side note to our beginning is that being from Michigan and going to school seven hundred miles from home, my mom was afraid I would marry some southern gentleman and run off, never to return. So, before she left me to spread my wings, she presented a tongue in cheek stipulation—I was only allowed to date guys from Michigan. I assured her I would do my best. After a few weeks of Chad and I being inseparable, I used the pay phone in my dorm building to call my parents and tell them the news. I proudly announced, "Hey Mom, I met this guy. He lives on Coon Hollow Road in Three Rivers, Michigan and he has a silver tooth!" There was a pause on the other end, then I heard her draw a resigned breath. "Okay, you can expand your territory into Illinois and Indiana." Needless to say, I did not take her advice. That was thirty years ago, and the rest is history!

That is our story of how we met. I wish we could sit across from each other over a cup of coffee and hear the beginning of your story about how you and your spouse came together. Each of our stories are as unique as our personalities and experiences. However, I'm certain even among our differences, one thing we have in common is that while good looks might have brought us together, they aren't enough to keep us together! Let's be honest—as time passes, we all change a little, so there has to be more than our initial attraction to carry us to lifelong satisfaction.

What is it that carries us from the butterfly stage to the grave? What bridges the gap? What keeps our marriage healthy and happy long after gravity sets in, the sparks fade, and the kids leave? After thirty years of marriage experience, Chad and I have discovered the answer is friendship. *Friendship is essential in building a lasting and happy marriage.*

Friendship is what gives our relationship the sustaining energy to go the distance and keeps us enjoying each other along the way. Rewind to your beginning again. Do you remember the fun you had and the butterflies you felt? For some, those feelings of "I can't wait until I see you again" and "I want to spend every waking minute with you" are still going strong, but for others, they have slowly faded. The good news is they do not have to be forgotten. When Chad and I reflect now on the beginning of our relationship, with our past experiences shaping our perspective, we clearly see how extremely important it is to continue developing our friendship.

It is interesting, however, that many of the books we have found on strengthening your marriage focus on how to rekindle passion, better communicate, or how to resolve conflict. While these are important, we don't find much on the importance of friendship, when it's the reason our wedding vows include, "To have and to hold." The vow promises more than affection, and it is not just beautiful poetry or a pointless pledge. The underlying meaning implies the bond of friendship is what gives marriage a strong, solid foundation.

The vow made perfect sense to the couples who were getting married during the early 1500's when these vows were originally written. The traditional wedding vows can be traced back to the medieval church in England and were compiled in a book called, "The Book of Common Prayer." Brides and Grooms in the Middle Ages understood that the phrase referred to something called "the habendum clause," which begins with "to have and to hold" and was a lawful definition describing a transfer of property. This legal bond implied ownership, rights, and belonging. The newlyweds easily translated the concept into relational terms—I belong to you and you belong to me; we are bonded together. Our modern definition is less about a legal bond of ownership and applies more to the emotional bond of friendship. Without the strong bond of friendship, any marriage can crumble and eventually collapse.

We have seen it time and again. There is a tendency once couples get married to no longer refer to their spouse as their best friend. They begin to take the friendship formed in the beginning of their relationship for granted and don't prioritize it like they used to. Date nights once held at their favorite Italian restaurant are now spent folding laundry and mowing the grass.

As life happens, it becomes easy to fall into our respective roles and settle into a routine without giving it much thought (especially after kids come along). Before you know it, our marriage covenant morphs into a business contract and our interactions become more about logistics than love. Our conversations that used to involve the sharing of our hopes, dreams, feelings, and future, digress into the practical: "Who is picking up the kids tonight?" "What time are we meeting your folks this weekend?" "Can you grab milk on your way home?"

No one neglects their friendship on purpose. It's not something we want to happen nor does it occur overnight, but we can easily drift apart and become two people who simply coexist, sharing the same address and toothbrush holder, if we aren't intentional about strengthening our friendship. Whether or not we have continued to develop a healthy friendship can be determined by our level of happiness, since friendship is also what enables us to enjoy marriage. We don't get married to simply endure the relationship. We got married because we enjoyed being with each other.

The good news is that strengthening our friendship with our spouse is not a new skill we need to learn; we all started our relationships as friends, remember? Rather, friendship is an aspect of our marriage we need to intentionally guard and grow. No matter where you are in your marriage, whether you are struggling or celebrating, we pray you find within these pages hope and help, energy and encouragement to strengthen your relationship so you enjoy a happier, healthier marriage.

Before we go any further, let's make sure we're on the same page. We should be clear and define what friendship is so we have a common understanding of what exactly we are talking about. You may be thinking of words that describe the qualities of a friend, such as supportive, respectful, caring, trustworthy, committed, and loyal, but how would you define friendship? In this book, we'll be using the following definition:

Friendship is an emotional bond between two people who feel accepted when vulnerable.

Very seldom does a couple begin sharing their deepest secrets on the first date. Most relationships follow a natural progression over time as we connect through commonalities like "Hey, you're from Michigan and I'm from Michigan." We take our time in this stage by figuring out our degree of compatibility and discovering shared interests. After we feel comfortable at that level, we begin sharing our thoughts, which eventually leads to disclosing what we feel. Divulging our feelings is the deepest level of vulnerability that happens gradually over time until we reveal, "This is who I am. This is the real me."

When we open up and display our true self and the other person responds with warmth and acceptance and it's a positive, pleasurable interaction, something special happens— a bond is created and we become emotionally connected. It is like a powerful magnetic force that we can't see with our eyes, but we feel in our hearts as we are being invisibly drawn together. The more we experience our interactions to be pleasurable and positive, the more we're going to take risks in being vulnerable. Each time we continue to be accepted, the bond continues to strengthen, and a positive cycle continues.

However, if we open up and share our true self and we're met with rejection—that is, if we're made to feel stupid for feeling the way we do or it turns into an argument—we'll naturally shut down and won't feel safe to open up next time. At best, the emotional bond is shorted, and at worst, it is severed. Who knew "falling in love" was so complex?

This is how God wired relationships to work. He is the one who came up with this intelligent design for marriage. As He was going along creating the entire world in all its brilliant detail, He kept saying, "It is good," up to the point when Adam was standing by himself in the middle of the Garden of Eden. God announced then and there that something was not good. He declared, "It's not good for the man to be alone. I will make a companion who will help him" (Genesis 2:18, NLT). His plan wasn't quite complete.

Almighty God remedied the situation by creating a beautiful woman named Eve with the intention that she and Adam would create a life bonded together as friends—a life lived in security, acceptance, freedom, and enjoyment where they were safe with each other. It was a perfect design as they were placed in a perfect environment. Even though we, as humans, have messed up a perfect plan, God's idea that marriage involves a husband and wife enjoying life, bonded together as friends, has not been altered. His desire for Adam and Eve in the beginning is the same for your marriage today.

The acronym SAFE can be used to describe the core components of friendship that give our marriages a strong foundation and keep us happy along the way. These components are Security, Acceptance, Freedom, and Enjoyment. Unfortunately, Chad and I learned these fundamentals the hard way.

We wish we didn't have to admit this, but there was a long span over several years when we weren't experiencing a safe and happy friendship in our marriage. We were in survival mode, trying to keep up with four kids in an eleven-year age span, running from this sporting event to the next. We felt like we were buried under laundry piles and stacks of bills. Both of us were continually on the defensive and tried controlling each other to get what we wanted. It was not any fun, and we did not enjoy being together! The underlying problem: we were not making our friendship a priority.

God took us through some difficult yet beneficial experiences to show us what a healthy and SAFE friendship looks like, and has brought us to a better, much healthier, place in our marriage. We learned by falling down and failing forward, which has only increased our desire to help others avoid the mistakes we made. As they say, hindsight is 20/20 and as we reflect on our journey, we discovered four qualities that are key components to friendship. When these elements come together, we experience a strong connection and enjoy each other's company. Our hope is you will, too!

2. Security

God, not my spouse, is the only one to meet my deepest need:

to be fully known and fully loved.

I used to tell people that I got married at age nineteen and had my first child when I was twenty years old. I'd leave out the part that these two events were only three months apart. After dating for two years with the intent to get married, I became pregnant at the end of my sophomore year of college. I was in denial for the first few months, but by mid-July my mom put the pieces together. She came into my bedroom one evening, sat down on the edge of my bed, and calmly said, "I've noticed you haven't been quite yourself since you came home from college. You sleep all the time and you're as hungry as a horse. My guess is that you're pregnant." I froze as she continued, "You'd better call Chad and tell him the cat's out of the bag." I was equally shocked and relieved as I took a deep breath and dialed Chad's number from the pink push button phone on my nightstand.

We wasted no time and within three weeks, my mom put our entire wedding together. She also gave me a crash course in Homemaking 101. I still have the recipe in my kitchen file on how to make mashed potatoes. That is how clueless I was, but the truth is I went from being a carefree teenager to a wife and mother rather quickly.

Our lives changed drastically and instead of signing up for fall classes, we signed an apartment lease. Both sets of parents encouraged Chad to finish school and get his degree, but I dropped out and took on a part-time job. I was used to being dependent on my parents to meet my every need, so I just naturally shifted that dependency onto Chad. I believed it was now his job to take care of me and make me happy. That was my youthful, nineteen-year-old emotional mindset that made perfect sense to me.

I was equally immature spiritually. While I grew up in a conservative, Christian home and was introduced to God at an early age, it took me a long time to understand what a personal relationship with Him looked like. At a young age, I developed a huge misconception about God, probably a combination of my personality and perception, but I believed He was all about rules and performance. If I behaved well, did good things, and followed the rules, then God loved me. So, when I came home after committing the "cardinal sin," I felt as if I wore a scarlet letter on my chest. I was so ashamed and thought God was extremely disappointed and therefore now rejected me. My limited understanding and incomplete knowledge of God's true character created a huge amount of insecurity that would wreak havoc in my life for years to come.

To avoid feeling the tremendous amount of shame that hung over me like a dark cloud, I tried hard to be the perfect wife, mom, daughter, friend . . . you name it. I kept thinking I could earn God's love again and get back in His good graces. I also mixed that notion with the expectation that Chad was supposed to meet my deepest needs, but it turned out to be a bad cocktail. The more I tried to earn from God and expect from Chad, I became more discontented, frustrated, and unhappy.

Shame led me down a dark road and abandoned me in a pit of depression. I couldn't function. I couldn't take care of my kids or be the wife and mother I wanted to be. Anxiety gripped me in daily activities like going to the grocery store. It felt like an overwhelming task that left me paralyzed. I was on large doses of antidepressants and heavy antipsychotic drugs to the point I would even sleep in the bleachers during our boys' football games.

It took many years of therapy, medication changes, and heavy doses of God's love for me to realize that security is an inside job. It doesn't come from anything external. I began to understand that "Jesus Loves Me" isn't simply a Sunday school song for little kids, but a massive bedrock of truth I could build my life upon. God tenderly showed me through His Word and His people that Psalm 23 is more than a quaint passage printed on bookmarks and funeral bulletins to comfort the grieving. It's really a beautiful and accurate description of the One person who can meet my longing for security. Each of us has in the depth of our soul a desire to be fully known and fully loved. And we are. By God. His Word tells us:

> "He has . . . planted eternity in the human heart [a mysterious longing which nothing under the sun can satisfy except God]" (Ecclesiastes 3:11, AMP).

God purposely created us with a need that only He can meet. We were created on purpose for a purpose, and that is to live fully alive, awakened to the God who loves us. He is our source of security; He alone can meet our heart's cry to be known and loved perfectly. Until we stop searching for that need to be met from someone or something in this world—our performance, our possessions, or our person—our hearts cannot find peace and rest, nor will we feel content or happy in our marriage.

God created marriage as a reflection of, not a substitute for, His love. We are simply mirroring to our spouse what God's love looks like. When we expect our spouse to satisfy our need for security, it weakens the bond of friendship. Our unrealistic expectation puts more pressure on our marriage than it is designed to hold. A marriage is only as healthy and strong as each individual partner. I am so thankful that early on Chad was emotionally and spiritually strong and understood this, but it took a long time for me to say goodbye to shame and embrace security in God. We were emotionally and spiritually unbalanced for many years, which weakened our relationship.

Placing my security along with my hope and expectations in God alone has brought such stability and strength to our marriage. As I spent time in God's Word learning about His character and personality, I began noticing how He made Himself evident in my life through the grace and kindness of others. Real love is the process of meeting needs, and as God continued to meet me at every step along the way, I slowly became aware and then grew certain that God loves me—the real me, not the me I present in public, or the me I want to be, or the me I think I am, but the real me. It's mind blowing that He knows my worst but loves me the best.

Security in God's perfect love empowers us to shove fear and shame out into the open where it has nowhere to hide, and ushers in contentment that takes up its quiet residence in our heart. Our inner world becomes peaceful. I'm no longer restless because my mysterious longing for security has been filled with God's love. I'm no longer expecting more from my spouse than he is able to give. And it has become much easier to focus on the positive—not only in myself, but in my marriage.

Security in God is the cornerstone everything in life and marriage rests upon. When we run to God and not our spouse to meet our deepest need for security, we become stronger spiritually, emotionally, and relationally. The stronger and more secure I become, the stronger and more secure my marriage becomes. To have a strong and healthy friendship, we must find our security in God alone.

3. Acceptance

Accepting God's love enables me to give love to my spouse.

Perhaps you are thinking what I thought for so long: I can't turn to God because I'm too ashamed of what I've done. I'm not the person I should be. Trust me, I get it. It took years for me to grasp the magnitude of the truth that God's love is not based on me; it is simply placed on me and there is nothing I can do to change that. God's love has nothing to do with what you've done, and everything to do with who He is and what He's done. Your actions, whether good or bad, do not determine His love for you. God loves you exactly the same on your worst days as He does on your best days. I know it sounds too good to be true.

Our human nature has a hard time wrapping our minds around the supernatural, but that does not change reality—God loves you unconditionally, just as you are, where you are. And He died to prove it.

Days before Jesus was led to the cross to be horrifically crucified, He poured out His heart to God the Father. It was an honest conversation that summarized the entire reason Jesus came to earth—to reveal the heart of the Father. We can eavesdrop into the conversation found in John 17 as Jesus presents His final request before His time on earth comes to a tragic end:

> "O righteous Father, the world doesn't know, but I do; and these disciples know you sent me. I have revealed you to them, and I will continue to do so. Then your love for me will be in them, and I will be in them."
>
> (John 17:25-26 NLT)

Accepting the truth that God loves me fills me with His love and enables my heart to freely pour love back out. Think of God's love like a tall glass of water that satisfies our empty, thirsty hearts. He offers it to everyone and wants nothing more than for us to simply receive it, enjoy it, and share it with our spouse and others. But if you have not accepted His free gift, you do not have much to share. You cannot give away what you do not have. I sure tried. I kept shoving it aside, rejecting yet attempting to earn God's love and come to Him on my terms instead of accepting His terms.

Author Christine Caine summarizes my experience and that of many others in her devotional book, Unshakeable: "Accepting as truth that God loves you unconditionally is profoundly difficult when you have lived your life as a performance-driven, accomplishment-oriented, earn-people's-acceptance woman. Plus, if you bear deep scars of being rejected in the past and if you have been filled with shame either by that experience or by choices you yourself made, you might find it hard to believe God loves you. You may also be battling true guilt (you are indeed guilty of something you shouldn't have done) or false guilt (feeling guilty for no legitimate reason) and are therefore keeping your distance from God."

For a beautiful story that captures what God's heart truly looks like, I encourage you to read Luke 15 in the Bible. It's one of my favorite passages. You might be familiar with this chapter about the prodigal son. If not, here is a brief summary:

> There once was a wealthy man who had two sons. The younger son was impulsive and had no desire to wait to receive his inheritance, so he asked his father to give it to him early. The father agreed and the son took the money, left home, and squandered it away on wild living. Soon after he ran out of money and options, he found a menial job working with pigs. He was in such dire straits that even the pig slop began to look appealing. The Bible points out that "when he came to his senses," he realized his father's servants ate better than what he was dining on, so he sucked up his pride, composed a speech, and rehearsed it all the way back home. It went like this: "Father, I have sinned against both heaven and you, and I am no longer worthy of being called your son." The Bible tells us, "But while he was still a long distance away, his father saw him

coming. Filled with love and compassion, he ran to his son, embraced him and kissed him." He did not get very far in his spiel because his father would not have it. Instead, he told the servants to get the party started because his son was home!

I love this story so much because I can relate to the prodigal son plodding his way home. I, too, took the walk of shame from my bedroom to the living room when I finally faced my father and told him I was pregnant. Our culture was different back then. Our situation was not ideal and frowned upon in certain social circles, so naturally I was devastated that I had disappointed my parents and brought shame on our family. But my dad responded like the father in the story, which beautifully illustrates how God's heart is about relationship, not rules or performance.

I will never forget sliding next to my dad on the couch, then bawling into his chest saying how sorry I was. I just kept repeating, "I'm such a failure. I'm such a failure." But in between my muffled sobs, my dad, with his arms around me, gently whispered, "Failure is an event; it's not a person." In hindsight, that moment was so surreal and beautiful, and one I wish I could revisit one hundred times over.

One of my biggest regrets is that I did not accept my father's response or believe what he said was true. I was so stuck in the pit of shame that I did not realize my dad's gracious words were like a rope offering to pull me out. I couldn't even see the extravagant gift being extended. Whether I was too emotional, ignorant, or prideful, I simply didn't allow God's love, demonstrated in that moment by my earthly father, to fill me up and free me from my guilt and shame. Regrettably, I rejected the gift.

Looking back, I believe if I had accepted that gift of grace, I could have moved forward in life, pouring forth from a full cup. I could have entered marriage with the capacity to love my husband with a refreshing flow instead of sparse dribbles. I could have been interacting with and responding to Chad in loving ways that strengthened our bond of friendship and spent time enjoying life and marriage so much more. Instead, I turned into a critical perfectionist that eventually had a nervous breakdown in the parking lot of our local mall. One early spring evening, I finally snapped. I lost all sense of rationale, got out of our minivan, and took off, bolting across the parking lot. I even tried to get in some random guy's truck! Chad was so startled and frightened; he had no choice but to call 911. Moments later an ambulance arrived on the scene and I was taken to the psychiatric ward of our local hospital where I was put on suicide watch for several weeks. I'm not going to lie—it was awful, and I was only allowed release by agreeing to outpatient therapy.

The next few years were rough, and as I mentioned, they were filled with bottles upon bottles of medication, endless doctors' appointments, and hours of intense counseling. The results from one psychological test said, "Kristen is a boiling cauldron of bitterness and misery." Wouldn't you love to be married to that person?! You can just imagine the repercussions it had on our marriage. My poor husband. This was taking a toll on both of us.

Thankfully, God didn't give up on me. He never withdrew His generous, incomprehensible offer. I applied what I learned in counseling and began to renew my mind with the truth found in the Bible. His Word soothed my aching soul and began to heal my hurt, lift my shame, and set me free. The more I understood what God is truly like and that His love means He forgives freely and does not condemn, my bitterness was replaced with His grace and my misery turned to joy.

I am eternally grateful God never stopped pursuing me. When I finally surrendered and accepted the truth about God, His supernatural love poured into me and filled my soul to the brim. And guess what happens when you have a full glass? What's inside spills out! Now instead of bitterness and misery spewing everywhere, love, joy, and kindness began to spill out, refreshing our marriage. There is no longer a dark cloud hanging over us. We went from surviving to thriving, and from tolerating each other to actually liking each other!

I do not like to dwell on those dark and depressing days, and I am very thankful they are a blur in our rearview mirror. I am simply sharing part of our story and experience as one example of the negative impact that can happen in marriage if we do not find our security and acceptance in God alone. Many different scenarios can be played out based on personalities and experiences. Some people can become negative and critical, always finding fault with their spouse, where others become fearful and self-protective. Addictions, defensiveness, being easily offended or sensitive, blame-shifting and never taking ownership of one's actions are all behaviors that form when we do not accept His love and allow it to quell the longing inside.

If you have been trying to relate to God on your own terms, thinking His love is based on your performance or that it's conditional, don't wait a minute longer! Stop rejecting and start accepting! All you need to do is accept the truth that He loves you . . . a lot! Accepting God's love enables us to give love. Not only does God's love strengthen your friendship, but it also allows freedom to enter in—our third component in a SAFE friendship. And now we are really gaining traction!

4. Freedom

When I find my security in God and accept His love, I free my

spouse from unrealistic expectations.

If I could look you straight in the eye, I would tell you that it took years and years for these truths to sink twelve inches from my head to my heart. Change and progress do not happen overnight. Growth is hard to recognize in the present moment, but if we just keep going, in time we will see results.

When I began to run to God for security and accept His love, the way my husband and I related to each other began to change. It was as if the reins I was holding onto so tightly slowly loosened in my grip. I was trying so hard to make Chad give me what only God could give. Once I opened my hand to receive His gift, my unrealistic expectations dropped to the ground and shattered like a fragile glass figurine. Freedom entered in, swept up the pieces, and took up residence as the new sheriff in town! Our marriage would have a new way of doing things now.

When our soul is content on the inside, it creates freedom on the outside that reflects in our relationships. The burden of expectation is lifted as we give our spouse the space to be themselves without trying to get something from them. We no longer feel the desire to manipulate this ill-equipped human to meet our deepest need of being fully known and fully loved. The good news is, you will see a change occur when one spouse runs to God—but when both partners accept His love and find security in Him, your marriage will totally transform and others will begin to take notice.

People in your circle will recognize something unique about the two of you that whets their appetite for more, and will move closer to find out what it is. They might not be able to put their finger on it, but they'll say things like: "They have a mutual respect for each other." "They are best friends." "They really support each other's interests." "They seem genuinely happy for one another." "There is an easy feeling to their marriage."

What people are really pointing out is the freedom that exists—which is the total opposite of control. Control is making the other person responsible to meet your needs and expectations. That is restriction, not freedom! And if I am expected to meet a need I am not designed or equipped to fulfill, that creates a pressure that causes stress and weakens the emotional bond of friendship. A healthy, strong friendship simply cannot exist without freedom.

Let's take a quick look at 1 Corinthians 13:4-7 (NLT) to see what freedom looks like:

"Love is patient and kind. Love is not jealous or boastful or proud or rude. Love does not demand its own way. Love is not irritable, and it keeps no record of when it has been wronged. It is never glad about injustice but rejoices whenever the truth wins out. Love never gives up, never loses faith, is always hopeful and endures through every circumstance."

Nowhere does it say, "Love controls." If there is one surefire way to destroy a friendship, it's through control. However, we don't often recognize it because it comes in so many forms:

Guilt. Guilt is a typical way to control our spouse. It becomes evident when we say things like, "If you really loved me, you would . . ."

Anger. Frustration and disappointment from unmet expectations simmer for too long and reach a boiling point. We erupt. Anger is our basic protest that we can't control reality, so we bottle up or blow up. We become sarcastic and make cutting remarks which, instead of strengthening, damage our friendship.

Pushing Boundaries. We notice control when one spouse makes persistent assaults on the other person's boundaries. Like a strong-willed child throwing a temper tantrum or a persistent salesperson, one partner will throw a fit or argue and plead in an attempt to change the other person's mind until they eventually wear down and cave in.

Silent Treatment. Perhaps the most powerful attempt to control our spouse is when we withhold love by using the silent treatment. When we use love as a bargaining chip and keep it to ourselves until the other person does what we want, we are putting extreme pressure on our partner to do anything to connect with the one they love. It is the ultimate form of rejection as it essentially attacks the very core of our being. The silent treatment is a silent killer to freedom and friendship in marriage.

As you glance over the above list of actions, consider what these tendencies really are: selfish, childish, manipulative behaviors. We might have been kids when we got married, but we cannot stay kids and continue in marriage acting that way. We need to grow up! Onetime years ago I was so mad at Chad (I can't remember why) that I dug through the trash, pulled out a dirty diaper, threw it in a paper bag, and left it on the front seat of his car with a note that said, "Have a crappy day!" How mature is that?! I needed to grow up and act like an adult. Mature adults take ownership and responsibility so freedom can grow in their marriage.

A mature adult can do all the things a strong and healthy friendship requires, like giving and receiving love, being independent, living out their values honestly, taking responsibility, having self-confidence, dealing with problems, developing their talents, and reaching their full potential. That is what a mature grown-up looks like. Ironically, that is also what freedom in a marriage looks like.

Galatians 6:5 says it this way: "For each one should carry their own load." To grow up we must put down our desire to control and pick up our own load. We are responsible to each other but not for each other. We can help each other out and hold each other accountable, but we are not responsible for the other person's load.

It's as if God gave each of us our own "bag" and we are to take care of what's in it. I'm responsible for my bag, and Chad is responsible for what's in his bag. If I start trying to dig in his bag or he tries to assume responsibility for what's in mine, we restrict each other's freedom and prohibit personal growth by taking responsibility for what is theirs. Like the commercial that asks, "What is in your wallet?" let's ask ourselves, "What's in my bag?" We need to know what we are responsible for. Here is a short, briefly defined list:

Feelings: One couple we know abides by the marriage motto: "I am 100% responsible to communicate my needs and feelings." They are on point! If you do not express what you need and how you feel, you will be miserable and constantly frustrated with your spouse because they cannot read your mind. Your feelings are a direct reflection of your thoughts, and even though your spouse knows you well, he/she does not know what you are thinking at any given moment.

Attitude: Just as my feelings reflect my thoughts, my attitude reflects my focus. If I am focusing on the positive qualities about my spouse and looking for things to be thankful for, my attitude is usually pretty upbeat. My husband is not responsible for my attitude, nor is my attitude dependent upon him. My attitude is up to me, so I need to make the choice daily—sometimes hourly—to be aware of what I am focusing on.

Choices: The power of choice is the basis for freedom. If you are constantly telling your spouse what to do and how to do it, that's not leaving them with the power of choice. You are suffocating them and taking away their basic individual God-given right, which will cause your friendship to deteriorate.

Time: Each of us has the same amount of time in the day. If we mismanage our time or can't say no to the point we overcommit, our marriage can suffer. If our partner feels like they are not a priority, the emotional bond of friendship weakens.

Talents: We innately possess God-given gifts that are meant to be developed and shared within our sphere of influence. We are acting responsibly when we carve out time to grow and reach our full potential. A gift I possess is writing. No one can tie my foot to a chair or tell me I can't write; it's up to me to take the responsibility to develop my skills for God's glory.

True freedom allows a spouse the space to responsibly and individually manage their own bag, and to communicate if they start feeling threatened to the point where the relationship is suffering. "Stop reaching in my bag" is an effective phrase we use that indicates a threat. Immediately it signals we have crossed a line.

Can you just imagine how much frustration, miscommunication, conflict, and even divorce could be avoided if we put down the desire to control and picked up and carried our own load? What would our marriages look like if we took responsibility for ourselves and our growth and stopped trying to manipulate and control our spouse? Not only do the negatives decrease, the positives increase. When freedom exists in your relationship, you can really ENJOY each other!

5. Enjoyment

When I am Secure, Accepting God's love, and Free, I can ENJOY

my spouse.

Chad used to say to me, "I know you love me, but I don't think you like me!" I was so hung up on trying to control him that I couldn't enjoy him. Performance pressure decreases the fun factor in marriage, and mutual enjoyment is what makes marriage worthwhile! Do you ever notice couples meandering through the grocery store who look like they are just miserable? I think it was those couples who came up with these one-liners about marriage:

> *"I've been married for 25 years and they've been 10 of the best years of my life."*

"My wife and I were happy for 20 years, and then we met."

"Love is blind but marriage is a real eye-opener!"

"If you can't say something nice, say it to your spouse; they aren't listening anyway."

"Marriage is finding that one special person you can annoy for the rest of your life."

Who wants to go through marriage being miserable together? Not me! I doubt you do, either. Most of all, God doesn't want that for us and He clearly says so in the book of Ecclesiastes through the words of Solomon, the wisest man who ever lived:

"Enjoy life with your wife, whom you love, all the days . . . that God has given you under the sun." (Ecclesiastes 9:9, NIV).

We didn't get married to simply coexist or at best tolerate this person for the sake of convenience. We chose to spend the rest of our lives with them because they were our best friend who brought joy to our lives! That sense of delight wasn't intended to digress into a sense of duty. I'm not trying to paint an unrealistic picture that every day should be like a romantic sitcom, but on the flip side, we can't let our marriage grow boring and stale either. Having fun together is essential, not extra.

As I've mentioned, there have been definite seasons in our marriage where we've completely neglected this area. Sadly, we felt like it was a frivolous luxury to go have fun together. Life demands that we work hard, be responsible, put the kids first, take care of the urgent all while ignoring the important— our number one human relationship.

The notion that it takes money to enjoy each other was another deterrent for us. We lived on one income with four kids and did not have a lot of extra cash for extravagant date nights. We did the typical dinner at a local restaurant and movie thing, but I'm ashamed to admit that secretly I always wanted more. I wanted to be whisked away on weekend excursions that took me to faraway places. Early in our marriage we did not have social media that revealed what other couples were doing, so we were blissfully ignorant. However, when Facebook burst onto the scene, it ushered in a greater level of comparison and discontent.

Suddenly what we were doing wasn't as fun as what "they" were doing. I saw friends enjoying an evening on their pontoon while we sat on our patio. Pictures taken at fancy restaurants made our date night at Applebee's taste bland. When I look back, though, we did fun things. It's just that I didn't enjoy them or my husband because I was too busy making him responsible for meeting my ridiculous expectations that led to resentment and lack of enjoyment. I'm happy to think of how far we've come over the years. Now an evening riding our golf cart in the woods is so much fun to me. It's not what we do or how much money we have, but enjoying a healthy relationship that matters.

Our daughter-in-law, Hannah, has the sweetest grandparents, Nana and Papa Bob, who are a wonderful example of a couple who simply enjoy each other. They are both in their 80's but each is sharp as a tack and have more energy than me on most days! One of the things they love to do together is to ride their motorcycle. They are hardcore enthusiasts and think nothing of hopping on their motorcycle and riding three to four hours just to take our son, Alex, and Hannah out to lunch. They even took a cross-country trip while in their twilight years!

They also have the best sense of humor. For Christmas one year, Nana had a shirt made for Papa Bob to wear while on their bike. On the back was printed, "If you can read this, June fell off!" They are the perfect example of a couple who are still enjoying each other's company, even after more than fifty years of marriage. That is what I want our marriage to look like.

As you reflect back on your own journey, what are some of the fun things you enjoyed doing together when you began dating? Do you still do them? If so, great! If not, why did you stop? Chad and I used hike in the Blue Ridge Mountains of Virginia, but since we now live in the Midwest, we can't do that anymore. We do love driving to Lake Michigan, though, and taking in another part of God's beautiful creation. Kayaking, wandering around a bookstore, riding in our golf cart, playing games at the kitchen table, or watching Netflix are what we enjoy most.

The struggle is real. We get it. Life happens. Kids and careers, responsibilities and routines can creep in and steal our time, but we don't have to be taken hostage and held captive to alternative agendas. The fun factor increases when you become intentional about spending time together doing things you both enjoy. Maybe it has been so long since you've enjoyed doing something together that it is time to find a new activity. Initiate it, plan it, schedule it. Having fun while enjoying each other's company is just as important as the other three qualities of a SAFE friendship. Fun and adventure aren't just for newlyweds. They are essential and give our marriage the strength and energy to last until death do us part.

To Have and To Hold

"To have and to hold" is the wedding vow that reminds us how we bonded together in the beginning. Its significance bids us to remember that we began our journey as friends, and that emotional bond is what will carry us until death do us part.

Did you notice how each component of friendship builds upon the next? When we go to God, not our spouse, to have our deepest need of being fully known and fully loved met, we become secure. We no longer make our spouse responsible to fill the hole in our heart that only God can fill. Pursuing the love of God is a worthy life quest that will significantly impact your marriage. We will never reach the end, which is as deep and wide as the ocean, but we won't waste a second of our life immersing ourselves in the vastness of it, either. There is so much more to life than what this world offers. God's love lasts into eternity and He, not our spouse, is our only source of security.

When we're secure and accept God's love, we have love to give away. I shake my head with a profound sense of sadness to think of all the wasted years I spent trying to earn what I'd already been so freely given. His gracious offer extends to every single person on this planet. We've been conditioned to believe that if something sounds too good to be true, it probably is— but that's the essence of why the gospel is called the "good news"! The good news is that when we receive the love and salvation God extends through His Son, Jesus Christ, we are rebirthed into His family. We become His children. He loves us unconditionally and fills us completely with Himself. The more we pour out, the more we find we never run out.

Security and acceptance extend an invitation for freedom to enter our marriage because we no longer feel the desire to control our spouse. We release them from unrealistic expectations that weaken our bond of friendship. I am not going to sugarcoat it, this takes work. It requires intentionality. But the payoff is so rewarding! We experience the internal peace and joy that affects our external circumstances and number one relationship on earth. Our marriage becomes stronger and healthier in ways we never dreamed it could. Critical, contemptuous, and downright nagging behavior morphs into positive, respectful, and supportive comments and actions. Turning to God and taking responsibility for our own growth is the best, most transformational and freeing thing we can do for our marriage.

Once we are free, we can ENJOY each other and find mutual satisfaction as best friends! We actually like each other and cherish time just being together, sometimes while doing nothing. I still enjoy time with my girlfriends and Chad looks forward to hunting season with his buddies, but there's no other relationship on earth like the bond of friendship between husband and wife.

God didn't design marriage to be monotonous or mundane. Marriage is meant to be full of laughter, fun, and enjoyment that last a lifetime. A SAFE friendship is essential in building a strong and healthy marriage that we can have and hold.

6. Play Together

Let's close with a practical action step that will easily strengthen our friendship. It's straightforward, fun, and it's simply this: play together! Shared activity is the best way "to have and to hold" your spouse and strengthen your friendship. Here are a few simple suggestions that can make that happen:

Let Your Spouse Be Themselves. We all have a few quirks. Perhaps your spouse's quirks are what attracted you to them in the first place. When Chad and I first started dating, I had this weird ability to make a high-pitched screech that would get a dog's attention five miles away. When we were in large crowds and somehow lost track of each other, I'd make that noise and he'd know where to find me. It was funny to us, but not to those around me who felt like their eardrums were bleeding. Don't let the quirks that used to be funny morph into annoyances. Appreciating your spouse's uniqueness, quirks and all, lightens the relationship and opens the door for carefree fun and adventure! Speaking of adventure . . .

Be Adventurous. Why not add the element of adventure to your marriage? Pizza on the couch watching Netflix is fun, but so is driving go-karts at the local miniature golf center! Are you one to sit on a park bench and watch the wind create ripples on the river's water? What about packing a cooler, renting a kayak, and jumping in? Whatever you are used to doing, take it to the next level.

Say Yes. We don't always share our spouse's idea of fun, but developing the art of compromise and saying yes to trying sushi when you really want a half rack of ribs instead is part of a healthy relationship. Your spouse is active and wants to go rollerblading? Grab your elbow pads and give it a try. Even if you don't particularly enjoy the activity, you're being a good sport. Watching your partner enjoy themselves is sometimes better than having the fun yourself.

Lower Your Expectations. If you tend to think that date night should consist of fabulous candlelit dinners at expensive restaurants, attending the hottest concerts, or being whisked away to a lavish, luxurious Bed and Breakfast all the time, you will be sorely disappointed with miniature golf and kayaking! Life is not a 24/7 romantic comedy. Who knows, you may even get in a fight lacing up your rollerblades—but that does not mean you're doing it wrong or are not meant to be together. Happy couples who experience a strong friendship can have fun together even in the grocery store. It does not matter where you are or what you are doing but that you are together enjoying each other's company. Walking around your local hardware store and picking out a new bathroom faucet can be fun, just make sure you are not doing that for every date night! Be realistic. Be spontaneous. Sometimes you will have more fun than others, but that is what keeps marriage interesting!

Flirt for Fun. Playful flirting is fun! Start early in the day with texts saying how excited you are to be together later. Send little messages that encourage "late night" activities. Let your spouse know that you find them attractive, you enjoy being with them, and you're looking forward to holding hands during the movie, kissing in the car, and capping off the evening rolling around under the covers. Flirting is a great way to keep friendship fresh and leads to a deeper connection.

A SAFE friendship is essential in building a lasting, happy marriage and playing together is the best way "to have and to hold" our spouse for a lifetime.

Questions to Consider:

1. What attracted you to each other? Tell your spouse three things.

2. Which core quality of a SAFE (Secure, Accept, Free, Enjoy) friendship do you need to be intentional about developing? Which one would you like to see your spouse develop?

3. What is one new activity you'd like to try with your spouse? (Why not put it on the calendar right now?)

Notes:

II.

For Better or For Worse

Growing through Circumstances

We grow through troubling circumstances

when we apply God's wisdom to the

opportunities they present.

7. Trouble or Opportunity

If we were to draw a line down the middle of a piece of paper and write better on one side and worse on the other, then list the circumstances we've encountered in our marriages that fall under each category, our lists would be different, but we'd probably feel the same way. We welcome the "better" ones— the events like a newborn baby being placed in our arms, unlocking the front door to a new home, cheering from the bleachers as our child makes the game-winning shot . . . but what about the circumstances on the other side? Do we welcome those into our lives, too? We certainly did not welcome the amputation of our daughter's hand, my dad's long-term illness, Chad's father's tragic death on a motorcycle, my five-year battle with depression, or Chad's sudden job loss and layoff, to name a few.

The circumstances we consider "worse" are many times uninvited, unexpected, and uncontrollable. They are definitely disruptive to our life and marriage. These difficulties come from every direction and hit us like a sucker punch straight to the gut. Sometimes they are a result of our own dumb choices, but often we suffer from the actions of others. These troubling situations cause pain, conflict, frustration, and discouragement. No one in their right mind enjoys encountering challenging circumstances, but the truth is that we cannot avoid them. I do not mean to be Debbie Downer, but it is a fact of life that every couple at one time or another will encounter something that falls under the "worse" category. Unfortunately, it is just how this broken, fallen world works. It's also the reason our wedding vows include "for better or for worse" because both are part of life, and therefore, marriage.

We can't avoid them but what if, instead of looking at the trouble the circumstances cause, we look at the opportunities they present? I don't know about you, but when trouble comes knockin' on my door, I don't usually answer with a cheerful greeting and warm embrace. However, that's what Jesus's half-brother, James, is really encouraging us to do as he writes:

> *"Dear brothers and sisters, whenever trouble comes your way, let it be an opportunity for joy. For when your faith is tested, your endurance has a chance to grow. So let it grow, for when your endurance is fully developed, you will be strong in character and ready for anything."* (James 1:2-4, NLT)

James has stuffed so much powerful, marriage-building truth into this short segment of Scripture that it's worth taking a few minutes to unpack it. He starts out:

Dear brothers and sisters – At first glance, we may only see a customary greeting. However, looking further we realize this is an all-inclusive statement. It means the following message is for all of us. No one is exempt from trouble. No one gets a free pass. It is not "if you are good enough, rich enough, smart enough, strong enough, or generous enough," you will escape reality. James is clear that it is not an if, but when. That is why the next word is "whenever."

Whenever – James is reinforcing Jesus's statement made in John 16:33: "Here on earth you will have many trials and sorrows . . . ." So many people have the misconception that if you become a Christ-follower, your life and marriage will be perfect. We do such a disservice to others and set them up for frustration and failure when we portray the Christian life and marriage as peaceful and happy all the time. It's not! Instead, it's a journey of ups and downs where we ought to be motivated to seek and trust God in both. Social media can skew our perspective of reality as most people only post their highlights, using beautiful filters and leaving out the snapshots of their bad days. This incomplete picture of a person's life and marriage can create the notion in our minds that we are the only ones who struggle or have trouble. It can make us feel pushed to the fringe where we end up isolating ourselves, avoiding community. But the truth is, we all struggle. Every single one of us will encounter troubling circumstances in marriage.

The next phrase, however, is where we may go in different directions.

Let it be – These three little words imply we have a choice in how we respond to these circumstances. We have options. We can rebel against God, shake our fist, turn our back, and blame Him for the pain we are experiencing. We can muster up strength to push through on our own and do what we think best. We can give up under the pressure and run from the problem. We could sit around and complain to anyone who will listen. Or, we can take advantage of the opportunity that is being presented in the difficulty. Believe it or not, there is a good opportunity. It's the opportunity to grow and become fully developed, strong in character where we are stable, secure, steady, and self-disciplined—unshakable!

I was an emotional hot mess for a long time, and my instability negatively impacted my marriage. I was bitter and defensive, and couldn't handle any amount of criticism or stress. Chad would innocently enter the kitchen, pick up a spoon and stir the pot on the stove, and I'd blurt out, "You think I can't cook. I'm not good enough." He'd reply cautiously, "No, I'm just trying to help you." I struggled so badly with perfectionism that I never felt I was good at anything.

Perhaps you can relate, or maybe you struggle in other areas. Maybe you are prone to anger and have a bad temper or are stubborn, impatient, and critical. I'm not trying to step on toes! I'm just saying our weak areas that need growth can really put a strain on our marriage and are especially evident during difficult circumstances and seasons.

Thankfully, God loves us too much to leave us in our immaturity and weakness. He knows a strong and healthy marriage is dependent upon our personal growth. Our relationship is only going to be as strong and healthy as each of us are individually, so He is always moving us down the path of character development. When we are strong in character, we are able to experience God in greater measure, enjoy our marriage in deeper, more intimate ways, and our sphere of influence expands as others are drawn to our maturity and stability. When we are fully developed, James says, we are ready for anything!

Not only will we become stronger and capable of handling the difficult circumstances, but we will be able to enjoy and experience good things, too. God is a good Father and has plans for your marriage and your family. If He were to peel back the curtain of heaven and let you peek, you would not believe what He has planned. God has blessings He wishes to lavish on you and big dreams He cannot wait to turn into reality. He wants nothing more than for you to bask in His love and enjoy a fulfilling marriage, and He delights in watching you impact this world using your unique gifts. This is His heart toward His children.

God's Heart as a Good Father

It's important to keep in mind God's goodness and our growth as the double-sided goal while in the middle of our difficult circumstances, because it can be a struggle to see the loving hand of God through the blur of our tears. In these moments, we need to be reminded that God's love is not a pampering love, only after our comfort and ease, but a perfecting love—that of a good Father who is always working with our best interest, the growth of His children, at heart.

I've learned so much about the heart of God as I relate to my own children. Chad and I have four kids who are all so different in personality, but my heart toward each of them is the same. Do I want each one to have a blessed life, a good life, a full life? Of course! But that can only happen if they grow into mature adults who are responsible, relate well to others, reach their full potential, and have a rich relationship with God. Our children will not fully develop if we give them everything they want. If that were the case, they'd eat ice cream for dinner, stay up late playing video games, never do their homework, or get a job and move out because human nature pursues comfort. It's our default setting. We don't naturally pursue growth. It is my job as a loving parent to provide them with what they need to grow, so I guide, correct, discipline, and teach out of love because I want what is best for them. But they do not always like it.

My experience as a parent has also helped me understand that God does not enjoy seeing us struggle. I think of how I felt watching my children while they learned to tie their shoes and got all frustrated as each little loop and knot got tangled. I wanted to bend down and do it for them, but I knew once they got it, they'd reach a new level of maturity and feel the sense of accomplishment that would serve them well. Our loving heavenly Father has a similar perspective, yet one that is infinitely beyond our limited understanding. He knows that our greatest troubles birth some of our greatest blessings, and that our struggles produce strength.

This is certainly true for Chad and me through the years of our marriage. We can honestly say that we are living our best life now because of our difficult circumstances. The lessons we learned and the strength we gained through our challenges have served to grow us individually, grow us together, and deepen our relationship with God. I like to say that I got a Master's degree from The School of Hard Knocks. We learned some lessons the hard way, but nonetheless, we learned.

While we may not be able to control these uninvited, unwelcomed circumstances, we can control our response. We can let them make us bitter or better. Instead of looking at the trouble they cause, we can choose to look at the opportunity they present and as a result grow through, not just go through, them. We can allow them to make us become strong in character, ready for anything! But how? I'm glad you asked!

8. Get Wisdom!

To go through or grow through? That is the question!

Can we be real and admit we need help to grow through our difficulties? Difficult circumstances are, last I checked . . . difficult! They are hard, challenging, tough, uncomfortable, and they carry with them a lot of potential to disrupt our status quo. Difficulties can sometimes shake us emotionally to the point where it's hard to think and act rationally. They make us frustrated and confused because doing what we've always done isn't working, and quite frankly—it could be that we've never encountered a situation like this before, so how are we supposed to know what to do or how to act?

May I suggest that the most uncomfortable thing about difficulties and why we dislike them so much is because they reveal what's inside. Trouble has the capacity to expose our weaknesses and show what we're made of—as individuals and within our marriage. Chad and I live in southwest Michigan, a region with flat farmland prone to destructive straight-line winds. One year a fierce storm blew through and ripped off the entire front of a house not far from us. Nothing else around it was damaged, but the remaining structure looked like a life-sized doll house. You could see everything inside just as it was before the storm came.

The brutal winds of troubling circumstances do the same to the façade of our marriage and expose what is really going on in our relationship. While our tendency is to run for cover and hide, it's not a bad thing or sign of weakness to be open and honest, and admit that we need help navigating difficulties. In fact, if we keep reading, James assumes we need help. The very next phrase after "strong in character and ready for anything" says:

> *"If any of you lacks wisdom [to guide him through a*
>
> *decision or circumstance], he is to ask of [our*
>
> *benevolent] God, who gives to everyone generously and*

without rebuke or blame, and it will be given to him."

(James 1:5, AMP)

James gets right to the point: "You need help. Here's what to do: ask for wisdom." It's wisdom that will help us grow from Point A, our struggle, to Point B, our strength. Wisdom will help us navigate from "worse" to "better"! As we ponder James's encouragement to seek wisdom, three questions arise that we should quickly address, because they will help clarify what can seem like a vague concept. Here they are:

1. **Why wisdom?** (Why didn't James suggest that we ask for grace, strength, or patience?)

2. **What is wisdom?** (What are we asking for exactly?)

3. If the Scripture says it will be given to anyone who asks, **how do we receive it?**

Why Wisdom?

In our search for answers, let us go to the Book of Wisdom, also called Proverbs, which written by King Solomon, who God considers the wisest man to ever live. Solomon dedicates the book to his son as he expresses his heart with a sense of urgency. Solomon implores his son to "get wisdom, for it's the most important thing you can do!" If you read through the entire book, you will see the word "wisdom" appear 48 times in 31 chapters. He explains that wisdom possesses tremendous value because it acts as a flashing, neon sign pointing us in the right direction as we journey through life.

When we find ourselves in those inevitable difficult circumstances, it's wisdom that enables us to make good decisions that allow us to enjoy life, while escaping the consequences from choices we later wish we could undo. I don't know about you, but I frequently wish I could undo choices I've made in life. I'm often tempted to write a book based on a quote I saw on a bumper sticker: "Don't follow me, I do stupid stuff!" Some of us just learn the hard way, I guess—which is why we need wisdom. But what exactly is it?

What is Wisdom?

Wisdom is the God-given ability to make the best possible choice for the best possible outcome.

Isn't that what we want to do in our difficult circumstances? We stay up late, tossing and turning because we are trying to figure out the best solution to what it is we are facing. No one wants to make a dumb decision to make a difficult circumstance more challenging! We may think we know what's best, but truly only God knows. That is why it is important to seek Him as He imparts wisdom through His Spirit, who allows us to see things more clearly than we perceive with our senses.

We are able to recognize wisdom when our head and heart come together. It is essentially knowledge combined with understanding—we know the facts, but also understand the multiple facets of the situation and rely on the Holy Spirit to help us make the best possible choice for the best possible result. When we understand what wisdom is and why we need it so badly, the next logical question presents itself: "How do we receive wisdom?"

How Do We Receive Wisdom?

God dispenses wisdom in a variety of ways that we may not always recognize it right away, but we can be sure He will not keep it a secret from us. The two primary ways He communicates are through His Word and through His Spirit.

1. **A Specific Word from Scripture** – This is why it is important that we carve out time daily to spend in His Word. When we need help regarding a relationship, work situation, or something affecting our kids, He'll lead us to a specific verse or story that gives insight to our situation. Wisdom written on the pages of Scripture comes in two forms: it is either concrete or in context. If it is concrete, it is a direct command: "Do this," or "Don't do this." Context is when the passage or story reveals God's heart, highlights human behavior and interactions, or gives examples of people in different situations where we can learn from their experience. Sometimes the words seem to jump off the page even though we might have read them one hundred times before, because this time relates to what we're going through.

2. **His Spirit** – One role of the Holy Spirit is to provide our inner being with a measure of peace or to alert us with a halting sense that makes us cautious to proceed. People sometimes refer to this as a "gut instinct" without giving credit where

credit is due, namely that it is God's Spirit speaking to us. Like an internal alarm, He will alert us to something that will ultimately hurt us, like an unhealthy relationship, or an unethical business deal or financial decision. Other times, we may have ideas, thoughts, phrases, or songs that spontaneously pop into our minds to help us see clearly. These instances could also be God imparting wisdom through His Spirit.

God gives His wisdom in other ways, too. He speaks through the world and people He created. There have been times I have crossed paths with a certain person who says the right thing at the right time. You could say it's a coincidence, but is it really? God also uses our spouse to speak truth and wisdom. He uses their perspective, discernment, and insight to guide and direct us, even though we may not always like admitting they have a point!

We can be confident and believe God will freely give us wisdom when we ask, we just need to be aware and expectant. It's easy to focus on the problem when we are going through a difficult circumstance, but if we fix our eyes on the One who has the solution, we can believe we'll experience the best result

in the end!

The next time you encounter a difficult situation, my

encouragement is for you to not let the storm blow you down,

but grow you up. We grow through our circumstances when we

apply wisdom to the opportunities they present.

When I was a young mother and my baby boy was sick, I

took him to the doctor. The doctor checked him over, then

diagnosed an ear infection. He handed the prescription to me

and spoke in a slow and condescending way: "This medication

is taken orally, which means it's by mouth. He should get better

within a few days. If he doesn't, come back. Do you

understand?"

I was offended and remarked snidely, "I know how to give

my baby medicine." His tone softened a bit as he explained,

"Well, I had a mother in here who had a baby with the same

ear infection, and I didn't clearly explain the instructions. Her

baby wasn't getting any better and when she brought him back

in, I knew why. He had pink crusty junk in his ears. She put the medicine in his ear when she should have given it to him by mouth!"

Wisdom is our prescription in difficult circumstances, and when we apply it properly, we will get the best result. So, instead of focusing on the trouble our difficult circumstances cause, let us look at three specific growth opportunities they present and how we can apply wisdom by reflecting on the lives of an historical, well-known couple found in the Bible. Can you think of who they might be?

9. Examine Ourselves

Mr. and Mrs. Job

I cannot think of a couple, past or present, that has encountered more troubling circumstances in one day than most of us (God help us) will experience in a lifetime. The book of Job is named after the husband, but we can safely conclude his wife was right there with him undergoing the same horrors. You might be familiar with their tragic story.

The Bible describes Job as a man of complete integrity. He was well respected by everyone and he feared God and stayed away from evil. He had ten children and was the richest man in his entire area. And in one day, Job lost it all. All of his donkeys and oxen were stolen, and his farm hands were killed. A fire fell from heaven and burned up all the sheep and shepherds. A band of raiders stole his many camels and killed his servants. Yet worst of all, his ten children were all having dinner together and a powerful wind swept in from the desert and hit the house. The house collapsed and killed everyone inside.

Job experienced more trauma and grief than anyone can possibly imagine, but it's his response to these terrible circumstances that is so shocking. Upon hearing all this tragic news, Scripture says,

> "Job stood up and tore his robe in grief. Then he shaved his head and fell to the ground to worship. He said, 'I came naked from my mother's womb and I will be naked when I leave. The LORD gave me what I had, and the LORD has taken it away. Praise the name of the LORD!' In all of this, Job did not sin by blaming God." (Job 1:20-22 NLT)

Woah. No wonder God chose to include his story in Scripture! That is a remarkable response and shows us the first opportunity troubling circumstances present us with: the opportunity to examine ourselves.

May I save you thousands of dollars and share something I learned through years of counseling? When we encounter difficult circumstances, what we believe about God, about life, about ourselves, and about our marriage will be exposed through our behavior. Like a tube of toothpaste when squeezed, what's inside will come out. Our core beliefs determine our response. If our beliefs are healthy and align with God's Word and His heart, they will allow us to respond in the best possible way that will help, not unnecessarily hurt, the situation. The reverse is also true. If we have unhealthy core beliefs, we will respond negatively to our circumstances.

In Job's case, these devastating events came out of nowhere and destroyed every possession Job had, but they didn't touch Job's faith. When everything around Job collapsed, his belief in God did not. This does not mean that Job did not struggle and wrestle with questions, but ultimately, in his soul, he trusted that God was still good and in control. This healthy belief served him well in the end.

I remember sitting in the hospital room with our daughter who had been through a tremendous amount of pain and suffering in the span of three short weeks, only to find out after ten lengthy surgeries during that time that her hand would have to be amputated. I can assure you, when you see your child in pain, you feel all sorts of emotions that range from anger to despair, and you'd do anything to take that pain away. Chad and I would have given our right hand for hers if that would have been the answer. But here we found ourselves seated next to her as she lay in a hospital bed, sedated and sleeping. The room was dark, and the only sound was the beeping monitors. Lost in thought, I looked over and saw my husband with headphones on, listening to music with his hands raised, and tears streaming down his face. I could tell what song he was listening to by reading his lips. It was a well-known praise song that reiterated Job's sentiment of praising God during the storm. Chad had his hands lifted high with steely confidence in God's good character. It was a profound moment for me.

Chad's core belief about God was that He was good and still in control despite the tragic circumstances we were facing. That meant He could be trusted. As Chad drew on God's strength, I benefited from the overflow. His wise decision to trust God during that difficult time strengthened my faith. Looking back, I know beyond a shadow of a doubt it was God's strength pouring into Chad that pulled us through that terrible time. He kept us together when we could have been ripped apart.

As I already disclosed, I did not always have healthy core beliefs, especially when I was younger, which caused me to respond negatively in many situations. I shared about my battle with depression. During that time my mind was cloaked in darkness and I couldn't articulate my feelings to bring them to light. I did not understand where my inner angst was coming from until I sat down one day and read in John 10:10 about Jesus coming to give us a full and abundant life.

His words penetrated through my fog like a search light, and I dropped my Bible onto my lap. I was feeling very discouraged and worn out, and thought to myself, "I've been a 'Christian' all my life, but if this is where it gets me, I'm out. I'm miserable and I don't know why. I've tried to be good and do good. I'm either missing something or I'm not doing something right."

At that moment, I prayed an honest prayer and asked God, "If You truly died to give me a full, abundant life, will You show me how to get it?" He answered immediately with the wisdom from His Word as I turned to Romans 12:2, which says, "Let God transform you into a new person by changing the way you think." I believed that was somehow my answer, but I didn't quite understand, so I replied back to God, "What's wrong with the way I think?"

I didn't know it at the time, but would later realize that every single one of my core beliefs about myself, God, and my marriage were so negative and toxic, they were causing me to respond in unhealthy ways. What I believed about myself were lies of shame that stemmed from getting pregnant before I was married. I didn't just believe I did something wrong; I was certain something was wrong with me! I believed I was a complete failure due to my poor choice.

What I believed about God was just as poisonous. I believed I didn't deserve His love. I had to earn it somehow. I had to be good enough to be drawn back into His grace. And my core beliefs about my marriage were that it was Chad's fault for our scarce financial situation since I did not get to finish college, thus forfeiting my career aspirations. These toxic core beliefs went underground, turning into resentment, anger, and bitterness, severely impacting my marriage in negative ways.

My emotional and spiritual health caused the collapse of my physical health, and that was the beginning of the long road on which God began to change me from the inside out. He began changing the way I think as He poured forth wisdom through His Word in front of me and His Spirit inside of me. Slowly but surely, the truth began to set me free!

I can't stress enough the importance of having healthy core beliefs, because when you are married, what affects one, affects the other. There aren't enough exclamation points for me to describe just how much my misery spilled over onto Chad. You might have picked up this book with the expectation to find some tips on how to change your marriage, hoping when you read it you could underline it and show your spouse . . . but the truth is, if you want to change your marriage, you must begin by changing yourself! And difficult circumstances give us the opportunity to see areas where we need to grow.

Unknowingly, my journey toward healing and wholeness began with an honest prayer. I was asking God for wisdom as I desperately wanted help and change. Psalm 51:6 says,

"But you desire honesty from the heart so you can teach me to be wise in my innermost being."

Our innermost being, where our beliefs reside, can be likened to a garden. The previous owner of our home had planted two huge flower beds that I had no clue how to manage. That first spring after we moved in, I didn't know which plants were weeds and which were flowers. I waited to see what looked pretty and what looked like it didn't belong. After a few seasons of watching beautiful flowers appear, I knew what to keep and what to get rid of. In a similar way, some of our beliefs are flowers—they are healthy, true and right. But some of our core beliefs are like weeds—they can choke out the growth and wreak havoc. We need to nurture the flowers, pull out the weeds, and ask God, the Master Gardner, for wisdom to show us the difference between the two.

The growth opportunities presented in our difficult circumstances allow us to do a little self-examination. We can deny we have weaknesses and flaws, even sin, or confess by saying, "To grow is to admit I don't know! God, I need Your wisdom." It starts by taking the time to sit down and ask His Spirit for wisdom as you examine yourself in the mirror of His Word. Make note of what's going on inside your heart and be honest with yourself and with God. He already knows everything, so there's no sense in hiding anything. It can be as simple as, "God, You know what I'm going through. This is how I'm thinking and feeling. This is how I've acted or responded. Where do I need to change or what do I need to learn in this situation?"

A wise response in a difficult circumstance is to examine yourself. Be honest as you pour out your heart to God. Listen for an answer in His Word, from His Spirit, and from other people. Talk to your spouse. The chances are good that they have insights you could benefit from. You can be confident that God is there waiting to pour out wisdom to help guide you through the trouble and grow you into the person He made you to be. This leads us to our second growth opportunity our troubling circumstances present. Let's check back in with Job and his wife.

10. Explore Our Relationship

"Job scraped his skin with a piece of broken pottery as he sat among the ashes. His wife said to him, ``Are you still trying to maintain your integrity? Curse God and die' But Job replied. 'You talk like a foolish woman. Should we accept only good things from the hand of God and never anything bad?' So in all this, Job said nothing wrong." (Job 2:8-10 NLT)

As if it were even possible, Job's situation went from bad to worse. Shortly after the first set of tragic circumstances, he was struck with a terrible case of painful boils from head to toe, yet he still clung tightly to his faith in God. But his wife responded differently. She encouraged Job to curse God and die. Same set of circumstances, but totally different responses. Their beliefs collided, and it is not hard to imagine what happened next. After she told him he should just curse God and die and he called her a foolish woman, it is safe to assume there was relational tension and conflict! Seriously though, can you blame them?

When you are married you are one couple, but still two distinctly separate and different people who respond differently to situations. Being different from your spouse is not a bad thing. It is a good thing, a God thing. Our differences are neither right or wrong, good or bad, they are just . . . different! A green crayon is not better or worse than a purple crayon, and vice versa. Both are equal and both are good. The same is true in marriage.

Think of all the ways you and your spouse are different, starting with your personality. One of you might be an introvert and the other an extrovert. Where one spouse is the life of the party, the other is content to sit in the corner and talk to one person all night. You might be very scheduled, and your spouse quite spontaneous. Are you apt to do a quick U-turn to grab a donut while your spouse has their calories for the week all planned out? Do you feel free to speak your mind, but your spouse is more reserved, and you must ask a million questions just to know what they are thinking? Our personality differences are endless! Not only are we different in personality, to state the obvious, we also are different genders.

Many books have been written on this subject all coming to the same conclusion: we are as different as night and day! Men act on facts and women tend to respond according to their feelings. For example, if a friend asks me to do something I feel like I should do, but don't really want to, Chad will say, "Just tell her you can't do it." But I get all middle schooler-ish and worry how saying "no" will affect our friendship.

Another difference that you don't have to be married very long to discover is that men connect on a physical level, while women connect emotionally. I need to talk and share my feelings first, then I'm more likely to be interested in being physical, whereas Chad is much more open emotionally after we've been together sexually. Also, men are motivated when they feel respected, women are motivated when they feel cherished. My husband likes to think the only way I get in the mood is if he flexes his biceps, when honestly, a meaningful conversation can cause things to heat up!

We also handle stress differently. Men tend to withdraw, while women may need a good cry. The list goes on and on and because we are different in personality and gender, this causes us to think differently in the same situation. For example:

WIFE thinks: *He's always working because he doesn't want to be with me.*

HUSBAND thinks: *She doesn't appreciate how hard I work.*

WIFE thinks: *He doesn't want to help around the house.*

HUSBAND thinks: *I'd help more if she wouldn't demean me when I don't do it her way.*

HUSBAND thinks: *She's quiet tonight, so that must mean she doesn't want to talk.*

WIFE thinks: *He doesn't care enough to find out what's wrong.*

HUSBAND thinks: *My wife isn't interested in romance.*

WIFE thinks: *All he wants is sex.*

We are distinctly different in so many ways, but if we don't handle our differences in a healthy way, they can turn into divisions, especially in difficult circumstances. We become frustrated when our spouse doesn't see things like we do, and we waste so much time trying to change the other person when all we are doing is dividing apart. Instead, appreciating our differences will draw us closer.

When we grasp that being different is good because we each have an equal, valued perspective about the situation, positive change begins to happen. Conflict decreases and communication improves to where we can reach the middle ground of compromise. Our differences are meant to complement each other, not cause us to compete with one another, both attempting to get our own way.

One area where Chad and I are extremely different is how we approach parenting. After years spent in education, he concludes that kids, in general, are guilty until proven innocent. My 'mom heart' wants to believe the best about my kids, so I firmly trust they are innocent until proven guilty.

These two vastly different mindsets have caused much tension and conflict over the years. However, as I valued his perspective and he appreciated mine, we balanced each other out. We stopped fighting over who was "right" and who was "wrong," which allowed us to go behind closed doors and talk through the situation. We could work out a compromise in which the "punishment would fit the crime."

As we began appreciating our differences, we explored our relationship even further and discovered a wise thing to do: We learned to listen, and we listened to learn! Mark 4:24 encourages us this way: "And be sure to pay attention to what you hear. The more you do this, the more you will understand."

When we were hit with a situation that was troubling or saw the situation from different angles, we found the more we listened and tried to understand each other's perspective rather than interrupt and try to prove our point, we experienced positive results. This is hard to do in the heat of the moment, so we had to be intentional.

In the middle of the battle, most of us are already formulating a response before the other person is even finished. We're getting locked and loaded to fire our opinion, defend our position, or fix the problem. It takes effort and intentionality to learn to listen and listen to learn, but when you do, you'll gain new insight about the other person that deepens your understanding, draws you together, and grows your relationship. No wonder Jesus says it is an incredibly wise thing to do!

I doubt there has ever been a marriage counselor with someone sitting in their office complaining that their spouse listens too much. Can you imagine someone complaining, "He tries too hard to understand where I'm coming from." "She won't stop paying attention to my thoughts and ideas." "He's too patient when he processes what I'm saying." "She takes my feelings into consideration too often." Seriously?!

Another technique we discovered that helps us appreciate our differences is to follow up our listening by asking questions. Not to sound all therapist-y, but we use clarifying statements such as, "This is what I hear you saying. What do you mean by that? How do you feel about it? What's your take on this situation?" Listening to learn isn't a skill we develop overnight. It takes time and effort, but doing so helps us

appreciate our differences. It is a wise way to explore our

relationship and helps us to grow together, rather than get

pulled apart, during troubling times.

11. Expand Our View of God

"Then Job replied to God, 'I know that you can do anything and that no one can stop you. You ask who it is who has so foolishly denied your providence. It is I. I was talking about things I knew nothing about and did not understand, things far too wonderful for me. You said, 'Listen and I will speak! Let me put the questions to you! See if you can answer them!' But now I say, 'I had heard about you before, but now I have seen you, and I loathe myself and repent in dust and ashes.'"" (Job 42:1-6, NLT)

Upon hearing the disastrous news, Job's three friends show up to comfort him, which you would think would be a bright spot in his dark and gloomy situation. The men sat in silence for a few days, then the rest of the book records the questions, arguments, and heated debates between Job and his friends regarding the mystery of human suffering and pain.

I don't want to compare or downplay each of our struggles, but can you even imagine the level of pain that hit him so fast and hard all in one day? I can understand why he wrestles with questions and emotions and feels like God is nowhere to be found, because I have felt that way, too. I think it's normal and natural to have tough questions when disaster strikes. Finally, thirty-seven chapters later, God, out of a whirlwind, breaks the silence and responds with some tough questions for Job:

> *"Where were you when I laid the foundations of the earth?"*
>
> *"Who created a channel for the torrents of rain?"*
>
> *"Who laid out the path for the lightning?"*
>
> *"Have you given the horse its strength or cloaked its neck with a flowing mane?"*
>
> *"Is it at your command that an eagle rises to the heights to make its nest?"*
>
> *"Are you as strong as God and can you thunder with a voice like his?"*

When God finished speaking, Job answered (it's amazing he could even respond after all of that), "I had heard about you before, but now I have seen you with my own eyes. I take back everything I said, and I sit in dust and ashes to show my repentance" (Job 42:5-6). What's interesting about his statement is that Scripture says that in all of Job's questioning and wrestling, he never sinned in what he said about God . . . so what is he confessing?

Perhaps it's that his view of God was too small. In the middle of Job's extremely troubling circumstances wrought with heart-wrenching loss, overwhelming pain, immense grief, and aching loneliness, God revealed Himself to Job in such a powerful way that marked him deeply. The Creator of the universe who spoke the stars into existence also spoke to Job in a profound and personal way that was beyond anything he had ever experienced.

As a result, Job's faith in God expanded—it was deepened, strengthened, and ultimately rewarded! God blessed Job in the second half of his life more than the first, and the final verse says he lived 140 years after that—living to see four generations. He died an old man who lived a long, good life.

Job's example teaches us the wise response that grows our faith and expands our view of God is to run toward, not away from Him, in difficult times.

James 4:8 also encourages us in the same way: "Draw near to God and He will draw near to you." I'll never forget the experience I had the day my dad passed away. It was deeply personal, and the treasured memory is so special that it's tucked in my heart like an heirloom jewel kept in a velvet box. I had been anticipating the phone call for several weeks as my dad neared the end of his life, cut short due to kidney failure. He received a liver transplant when I was in high school and was told that the anti-rejection drugs he would have to take would eventually kill his kidneys. At best we could hope for fifteen years, and now, the time had expired. Like an unwanted bill collector, death was knocking on the door.

I lived about a hundred miles from my parents at the time, and after hanging up the phone upon receiving the dreaded news, I hopped in the car to go be with my mom. Most of the drive was a straight highway and I zoned out on the familiar road, oblivious to passing cars. It was the first of August, and the orange tiger lilies and tall lace-shaped weeds that lined the highway were a continual blur in my peripheral vision. I turned off the radio and was alone with my thoughts, when suddenly tears spilled down my cheeks and my sobs broke the silence.

I began crying out and asking, "Why, God? Why did you take my father so young—only fifty-nine years old with so much life to live?" I challenged God to a verbal wrestling match as I shouted questions that began with, "If You are good . . ." and ended with "I don't understand!" I cried out broken phrases and stuttered, my shoulders heaving: "I. Don't. Know. What. To. Believe. Anymore. God. Are. You. There?".

Unlike Job, I didn't hear a voice. God didn't answer me with a thunderous voice from above. The earth didn't quake, nor did a shining light appear and give me peace. Instead, a bright orange-and-black-winged monarch butterfly came out of nowhere and landed smack dab in the middle of my windshield. The bright insect snapped me to attention and interrupted my wails. I stared at this gentle beauty through the glass and was surprised the wind was not blowing it off. The heavenly messenger sat directly in my line of sight and softly opened and closed its wings, attempting to communicate with me. Each open and close of its translucent wings was like Morse code that I could not decipher. I was stunned.

I was about five miles from my destination and saw my exit ahead. I pulled off the highway and turned left onto the dirt road that led to my parents' home. The butterfly stayed with me until I pulled into the driveway. So bewildered, I turned off the ignition, sat in my car, and watched the butterfly take flight into the sky; confident it had completed its mission. Shaking my head, I pulled myself back to the present moment and went inside to find my mother.

The screen door slapped behind me and I saw her opening an envelope at the kitchen counter. She reached in and pulled out a little booklet. I gasped as I saw a bright orange butterfly on the cover. I walked over and read the title: There is life after death. I stopped in my tracks.

In my wrestling, wailing, crying, and questioning, God showed up. He didn't appear in person, but sent a little butterfly to do His bidding. My heart was so deeply and profoundly impacted that it still affects me to this day. Monarch butterfly sightings have become my Post-It notes from heaven, reminding me that God knows, sees, and cares. Through a little insect, my view of God expanded, and my faith was deepened in a personal and profound way.

Running toward God with our questions during difficult circumstances and inviting Him into our lives positions us to encounter Him in a personal and powerful way. Our soul receives His touch, and we are transformed from the inside out. Our heart experience changes our head knowledge. We begin to think differently as our faith grows and expands, so the next time we encounter trouble we can stop and remind ourselves, "God showed up and got us through that, and He'll get us through this."

As our faith grows, so does our character, which impacts our marriage. A single encounter in God's presence expands our view, deepens our faith, and leaves us better and stronger than we were before.

For Better or For Worse

We married "for better or for worse" and while we desire the better circumstances, reality is that we are all going to encounter the worse ones, too. While the struggle is real, we don't have to struggle alone. God is waiting for us to turn to Him and ask for help. We need wisdom, and we don't need to feel ashamed asking for and accepting support. God doesn't leave us helpless or hopeless. He gives us wisdom through His Word in front of us, His Spirit inside of us, and His creation around us. People, friends, and community are made to be His hands and feet with the words they speak and needs they meet. All we have to do is open ourselves up and do the next thing. It can feel risky, but it will be worth it.

Taking advantage of the distinct opportunities our difficult circumstances present us with looks different for each of us in our unique situations. Perhaps you find yourself spinning on the crazy cycle with your spouse. You keep going around and around the same issue, getting nowhere. Your ideas of what to do in the situation are completely different and causing frustration, making you mad at each other and even irritated at God. I get it. We have been there, done that . . .

plenty of times!

Asking God for wisdom can help you see the situation and your spouse differently, and as you learn to listen and listen to learn, you gain traction. No longer are you trying to defend your position; instead, you are seeking to understand your spouse in a deeper, more intentional way that leads to a level of intimacy you've never experienced before.

Be assured that God not only sees and understands your troubles, but He also knows how to lead you out of difficulty and into a place of prosperity, protection, and safety. You have His Word as a guarantee. The first chapter of Proverbs speaks to those who accept and those who reject His wisdom:

"Wisdom calls aloud in the street, she raises her voice in the public squares; in the gateways of the city she makes her speech. How long will you simple ones love your simple ways? If you had responded . . . I would have poured out my heart to you and made my thoughts known to you but since you rejected me when I called . . . calamity overtakes you like a storm . . . distress and trouble overwhelm you.

But whoever listens to me will live in safety and be at ease

without fear of harm."

Running to God with our questions, doubts, frustrations, anger, and disappointment is a wise decision. His patience is long, and His chest is big. He can handle your blows. It's okay to cry out in frustration; just don't turn away in rebellion. He is the only One who can handle our questions and calm our fears by giving us unexplainable peace amid a raging storm. The next time we're hit with a difficult "for worse" circumstance, let's not look at the trouble it causes, but the growth opportunities it presents.

12. Pray Together

The wisest action that has had the most positive, trans-formative growth effect in our marriage is our decision to pray together. I am talking just the two of us—not before meals with our kids around, although we do that, too—but private prayer where we open our hearts and put words to our thoughts and feelings. Sometimes Chad leads; other days, I start. One morning it could be 15 seconds, the next day it might be ten minutes. The amount of time will vary. The action is what achieves results. Praying as a couple draws us together and invites God into our everyday moments and chaotic messes.

Prayer has been called "The Great Exchange" because we exchange our burdens for God's blessings. We give God our problems and He gives us His peace. We have found that to be an accurate description and validated in Philippians 4:6: "Do not be anxious about anything, but in everything, by prayer and petition, with thanksgiving, present your requests to God. And the peace of God which transcends all understanding will guard your hearts and your minds in Christ Jesus."

Prayer ushers us into the presence of God where peace rules. When we pray, it's as if a sentry is standing guard outside the door and fear is not allowed inside. As we relinquish our anxiety to God in prayer, our benevolent Father replaces our worry with a deep-seated tranquility despite the raging storm that threatens to overwhelm us.

I'm reminded of a story in which two artists were asked to sketch a rendering that depicted peace. One artist painted a beautiful sunset with bright orange rays reaching down like arms trying to scoop up the vast, calm ocean. The other drew a bird sleeping on a nest situated in a tree that was being shaken by a storm. Rain and wind whipped the branches and caused the bough to sway, but the bird slept undisturbed. The latter is a more accurate picture of the peace God gives in the middle of our troubling circumstances.

Prayer is our connection to God and the way we communicate with Him. It is having a conversation with Him and expressing whatever comes to mind, just like you do with your spouse. Communication is the lifeblood to any relationship, and it's the same in our relationship with God. How can you have a connection with someone you never talk to? Your relationship will grow stale and stagnant without constant communication. Talking to God on a regular basis also keeps us closely connected to our spouse. Matthew 18:19-20 reminds us that God wants to be in the center of our marriage and help us overcome any challenges we may face:

"Again, I say to you, if two of you agree on earth about anything they ask, it will be done for them by the Father in heaven. For where two or three are gathered in my name, there I am in the midst of them."

By opening your relationship up to God and revealing your hearts to each other, you are growing closer and connecting on a deeper level, instead of dividing apart. You cannot hide your heart while praying aloud. Chad knows me well enough to detect when I'm just not feeling it. He knows when I am faking and just going through the motions. It is easy to disguise what is happening in my heart by hiding behind busyness. I can distract my husband by making myself appear calm, cool, and collected while flitting about in the kitchen or folding laundry. Our conversation is short and surface level and I can avoid revealing what is bothering me—most of the time, anyway. But when we come together in prayer, I have nothing to hide behind. My heart is naked and exposed, on display for my husband to see. I stand vulnerable to his questioning. Sometimes I find this irritating if I am holding back a confession; other times I find it comforting to know I have someone who cares enough to find out what is wrong. Praying together brings issues to light that, if remained locked away in the dark recesses of our hearts, have the potential to do some relational damage. It keeps us in check and accountable to each other.

Praying as a couple is how you fight for your marriage. It's amazing how prayer can soften a heart in a matter of minutes. I could be carrying around a grudge and playing out different scenarios in my mind on how I'm going to come at my husband, but suddenly, in the presence of the Holy Spirit, I'm convicted, and the tables are turned. Instead of focusing on the hurt or irritation, I see clearly where I am at fault in the situation. I am humbled and prompted to ask for forgiveness for my role. Prayer is a powerful weapon we can use to fight against the forces trying to divide us.

If praying with your spouse is something you've never done, don't be nervous or fearful. It will probably feel awkward at first and you might fumble and mumble in your efforts. Don't freak out! It's okay. Just talk to God like you are talking to your spouse. He encourages us to come boldly to His throne, where we will receive grace and mercy.

Together ask God for wisdom as you both examine yourselves. Look to His Word and listen to His Spirit. Ask Him to make you both wise in your inmost being, nurturing healthy beliefs. Ask Him for greater understanding as you listen to your spouse, appreciating your differences. The right words are not important because God knows what you are trying to say. He is simply delighted you are drawing close. He loves you and your spouse so much and wants to make Himself known to you in greater ways. When you ask, He will give you the wisdom you need to make the best possible choice for the best possible outcome! We know based on experience and the authority of His Word that He can use the absolute worst circumstances to strengthen, grow, and bring out the absolute BEST in you and your marriage!

We grow through our circumstances when we apply God's wisdom to the opportunities they present. Praying together draws us together, rather than dividing us apart, in difficult times.

Questions to Consider:

1. Which of the three opportunities resonated most with you and why?

2. Do you tend to run toward God or away from Him during difficult times? Why do you think you do that?

3. What situation are you currently facing (or have faced) that requires wisdom to make the best possible choice for the best possible outcome? Have you prayed about it? Why not ask God for wisdom right now?

Notes:

III.

For Richer or For Poorer

Uniting (Not Fighting!) Over Money

A couple becomes united when each spouse

values money as Jesus taught.

13. Misplaced Values

It wasn't one of my finer moments when, in my anger, I tore open a bag of hot dog buns and started chucking them at my husband across the kitchen. I don't recall what we were arguing about, but I do remember the flying hot dog buns and Chad running for cover as I yelled, "When I married Mr. Right, I didn't know his first name was Always!" Most likely we were fighting about money, because that seemed to be one of the top triggers for heated interactions early in our marriage.

We used to have knockdown, drag out fights over anything and everything. We'd argue over little pet peeves that included dirty dishes left in the sink and underwear on the bathroom floor to bigger issues like how to discipline the kids. We fought over where to spend the holidays, how much sex was normal, and what to cook for dinner. We worked through many of those issues in a timely manner but the one issue we couldn't seem to get a handle on was money.

We didn't have much when we got married. We started out behind the eight ball and, as my mom would say, "We didn't have two nickels to rub together." Our meager income did not even cover our apartment rent, so Chad's parents took care of that for us while he finished school and we both held part-time jobs. I worked in the evenings as a telemarketer and Chad was employed at a sporting goods store when he wasn't attending classes. Our minimum wage jobs helped us scrape by until Chad secured a teaching position, but even then, our kids qualified for free lunch at school.

We were thankful God always provided for our needs, but it seemed our finances never allowed for our wants. This caused me to get into some trouble with credit cards and I became quite clever in keeping my spending sprees a secret. I would go to great lengths to hide bags and rip off tags so Chad wouldn't notice when I bought something new. One afternoon

I was visiting my mom and remembered the credit card bill was due to arrive. I did not want Chad to get it before me, so I called and asked my neighbor to go over to our house and retrieve our mail! I shall let you use your imagination to fill in the blanks about what happened when Chad found out, but let me just say it was as if a grenade was thrown into our living room.

Show Me the Money!

Any Google search cites money as one of the top five reasons for marital conflict. Perhaps it's the reason our wedding vows include the phrase, "for richer or for poorer," because money is simply an inescapable and influential component in life. It affects everything—what you eat, where you live, what you drive, the clothes you wear, and how you spend your free time. It can also affect who your friends are. We would have loved to have taken luxurious spring break vacations with friends or thrown extravagant birthday parties for our kids. Instead we had many "staycations" and backyard birthday bashes that included five-dollar pizzas and water gun fights on the trampoline.

For being "just a piece of paper," money has an incredible power that dictates how you relate to and interact with your spouse. For much of our marriage, the subject was like the elephant in the room. Neither of us wanted to talk about it or even acknowledge its presence in our home. We just kind of danced around it, me especially. I would avoid the topic because our conversation would always turn into an argument or leave me feeling guilty about my spending habits. There really is no sugarcoating when it comes to money management in a marriage: If you do not unite, there will be fights!

In the "For Better or For Worse" section, we talked about how appreciating our differences helps us grow together. Well, when it comes to money, whether it's spending, saving, giving, or investing, we need to go beyond appreciating our differences. We must set them aside and become united. It is absolutely crucial we are on the same page. If we are working off different spreadsheets, there will be tension, conflict, frustration, and disagreement much like a road trip when Chad and I were trying to navigate using different GPS maps. He had Google Maps pulled up on his phone and I was using my Apple navigation system (programmed to speak in a cool Australian accent). My phone kept shouting at us to reroute and turn, while his was instructing us to go straight. Talk about stress! Once we decided to use one system we stopped arguing and arrived at our destination safely. There are certain areas of marriage you must be unified in—money and maps top the list!

However, unity does not mean uniformity. The goal isn't to think alike, but think together. We don't lose all sense of our individuality when we are united. We simply choose to set aside our own agendas and work toward one purpose. If I am saving for a beautiful home but Chad wants to build a nice nest egg for retirement, we are not unified in purpose and the result is a lose/lose scenario. Neither of us will get what we want, much less what God wants for our marriage. Paul stresses the importance of unity when he writes:

"Then make me truly happy by agreeing wholeheartedly with each other, loving one another, and working together with one mind and purpose." (Philippians 2:2 NLT)

Fake Couples, Real Scenarios

The only way we can be of the same mind and united in spirit when it comes to money is to share the same value system. Money itself is not the real problem because it's neither good nor bad. It is amoral. The value we place on money causes the problem. Some of us give it too much value. It can become our number one priority, and as a result, we make great sacrifices to get more at all costs. Others give it the wrong value and when we do, we find things don't go right in our marriage.

It might help to think of money like a campfire. When it's contained in the campfire pit, it serves a good purpose. It keeps us warm and brings enjoyment to our lives. However, sometimes we get the idea that a nice little fire is not enough, so we pour gas on it, which can explode and hurt someone. If a spark goes outside of the boundary, that can cause serious damage as well. We need to keep money in its rightful place, or it can cause big problems.

Allow me to explain further by using the following scenarios of fictional couples in what could easily be real-life scenarios. On the surface, it appears the couples are fighting over money, but if we take a closer look, we'll see the real problem is how they value money. Let's meet our first couple:

1. Rob and Angie – Rob is frustrated over how much his wife spent while shopping. Angie knows she didn't spend so much that they can't pay their bills, so she thinks, "What's the big deal? Why is he so upset?" Angie hasn't discovered the underlying issue. Rob perceives money, not God, as his source of security. He believes, "The more I make, the more I'm able to take care of things myself." He believes it's completely up to him to meet his family's needs, so he's frustrated over every dime that goes out because he's working so hard to bring—and keep—the dollars coming in! The issue is really about security. Rob values money, not God, as his source of security.

2. Tony and Shelly – This couple agreed upon an amount they would spend to purchase a used car. But upon arriving at the car lot, Tony laid eyes on a brand new, fully loaded, top-of-the-line truck with all the new bells and whistles (and it's way nicer than all his buddies' vehicles), so Tony has to have it. Despite Shelly's hesitation due to their previous agreement and her personal reasons against it, he tells the salesman they will take it. He does not care how much over budget it is because to him, this shiny, new truck is proof of his net worth, which to Tony equals his self-worth.

3. Bill and Karen – This older couple doesn't fight anymore because Bill has just given up. But they used to fight. In fact, they used to have family feuds equal to World War III, but those days are over. Bill doesn't say anything about his wife's excessive spending sprees because it doesn't do any good. He has realized Karen is just trying to numb the pain from the betrayal left by her ex-husband. She doesn't know how to heal the hurt or fill the void, so she constantly buys things to soothe the ache and feel high, much like a drug addict who needs a fix. Karen believes more stuff means less pain.

4. Greg and Melody – About every six weeks, this young wife gets after her husband because he works so much that he is never home to help with their three boys, all under the age of nine. She is tired of being a taxi driver, referee, cook, housekeeper, and on-call nurse 24/7. She'd like a break every now and then, but he's never around because to Greg, the bottom dollar is the bottom line. It is what life is all about!

"Show me the money" is his motto, and he will not let anything or anyone, namely his wife, get in the way of his money-making life mission.

Perhaps you can relate to one of these scenarios, or perhaps you have your own in mind. Each situation is played out differently based on the couple's value system. The first husband values money as his source of security, the second believes it determines his self-worth, Karen was convinced it is a remedy for pain relief, and the last guy, Greg, values money so much he made it his number one goal in life. He even prioritized it above his family. What seems to be the recurring theme or scenario that causes money conflicts in your marriage? Are you willing to admit you may be misplacing its value?

God's Purpose for Your Marriage and Your Money

God has a purpose for your marriage. He has dreams and work for you as a couple that revolve around helping people get to know Him better. The Apostle Paul points this out in several places in Scripture:

"He creates each of us by Christ Jesus to join him in the work he does, the good work he has gotten ready for us to do, work we had better be doing." (Ephesians 2:10, MSG)

"For it is God who works in you to will and act in order to fulfill His good purpose." (Philippians 2:13, NIV)

One of the coolest things about God's design for marriage is that He doesn't bring two people together for the benefit of just one. He knows every one of your differences and individual strengths and carefully combines them in such a way that you can accomplish more together than you could on your own. Before Eve was created, Adam already had a purpose. Adam was created to tend to the garden and care for the animals. The man had been given work to do. Yes, God created Eve for a relationship, but also to help Adam in his work. Back in Genesis 2 we read, "I will create a companion who will help him."

In God's brilliant two-fold design of a working relation-ship, He also built in a blessing; a measure of joy and satisfaction that results from doing the work together He has assigned. The original plan was that working together, unified in purpose, was to be a joy. Work only became cursed after the fall, when the first humans messed it up. But the closer we stick to God's original design, the more paradise is reclaimed and the more blessed we'll be.

I don't know about you, but I find it exciting and motivating to know that God's plans for our marriages are something we are uniquely designed for and will be blessed by doing together. You know who else understands this? Chip Gaines. Perhaps you've heard of him? He and his wife, Joanna, rose to fame through a hit TV show called Fixer Upper. Chip and Jo have a unique purpose that happens to be televised, but allow me to share a few paragraphs out of Chip's book that speak to the point I'm trying to make here:

"I am so keenly aware that God has entrusted us with Magnolia for a reason. This little company had always meant more to us that any amount of notoriety or recognition ever could. Magnolia will undoubtedly be an enduring part of what we leave behind. We pray that it will outlast us. We dream that our children's children will get to see what we've built, and it would be a monument symbolizing the value of finding joy in hard work.

Joanna and I also strive every day for the work that we do to create lasting, meaningful and positive change in our people and our community. We want our employees to rise up as leaders in their own right. We want them to follow their dreams, whatever they may be – go back to school and get that degree, become world-renowned in their fields or stay home with children, if that's what they feel they are called to do.

Even if the company loses our valued employees to these dreams of theirs, that's okay. It was our honor to be the runway for them, the launching pad that they needed to go for it. From there we're anticipating a chain reaction of sorts with exponential impact. We believe our employees will go on to change the world in ways that Jo and I could never attain by ourselves. Our legacy is their legacy and vice versa."

Talk about a guy who places value not in the money they have made, but on their purpose as a couple and the impact they have. Chip definitely gets it. We might not be created to become overnight design celebrities, but nonetheless, our purpose is of equal value to theirs. God wants you and your spouse to use your skills and passions, your money, and your resources to meet the needs of others and make an impact in the world. But here is the deal: if we want to become united as a couple, do the work God has called us to do, and fulfill our purpose as a couple, then each spouse must value money as Jesus taught.

When we understand how God values and views money, we can align our priorities to carry out His plans, which is to do the work He has called us to do. Proper money management from shared values will position us to fulfill His purpose for our marriage. Believe it or not, God has a lot to say about money. Jesus Himself talked about this subject more than any other topic in Scripture. Seeking His advice as our trusted financial advisor, we see four values emerge from His teaching:

1. **Money is not a true source of happiness.**

2. **Money is a test.**

3. **Money is temporary.**

4. **Money is a tool.**

14. Money is Not a True Source of Happiness

"Those who love money will never have enough. How absurd to think that wealth brings true happiness!" (Ecclesiastes 5:10b, NLT)

You've probably heard the saying, "Money isn't the key to happiness, but it can sure unlock a lot of doors." Or as our son Cameron says, "Money can't buy happiness, but it can buy a four-wheeler and I've never seen a sad person riding a four-wheeler." We can laugh because if we are honest, this idea is something we have all fallen for at times. We look at what we don't have and think we're missing out, so we frantically try to grasp and get more. It's like we live in a state of emergency, rushing to get to the ER, the place where things are biggER, bettER, fastER, richER . . . the place where we believe whole, happy lives are found. We have somehow attached our priorities to the word "more" and value money as the key to happiness, including a happy marriage. This toxic idea has seeped into our subconscious. We have been conditioned to believe that more money makes for a happier marriage.

But if we stop striving long enough and simply look around, there are plenty of examples of extremely wealthy couples who can disprove this notion, since they are now divorced. A quick internet search brings up, ironically, Google's co-founder, Sergey Brin, whose bank account even after his divorce is a whopping 50 BILLION dollars. Another couple is Amazon's founder Jeff Bezos and his ex-wife, MacKenzie, whose combined fortune hovers around 137 million dollars. (If 50 billion or 137 million can't buy happiness, no amount can!)

In the above verse found in Ecclesiastes, notice the word, "absurd." It's not a word we use regularly, but it means "ridiculous, irrational, illogical, silly, and strange." Absurd is an adult who still believes in Santa Claus or takes a shower and puts dirty underwear back on! I know it's not politically correct to call people absurd, but hey, I'm just the messenger delivering God's Word, which contains a wealth of knowledge, and it clearly says it's absurd to believe money is a source of true happiness.

Jesus Himself tells a story in Luke 12 about a man who believed that money could buy happiness and therefore decided to "take it easy and to eat, drink, and be merry!" Basically, he said, "My money has bought happiness! Life is good!" But wait. Look how Jesus concluded the story and how He describes this wealthy man:

> "Yes, a person is a fool to store up earthly wealth but not have a rich relationship with God." (Luke 12:21 NLT)

We've gone from absurd to straight up fool by thinking money can buy happiness. True happiness is only found in a rich relationship with God. I have learned from experience and can now recognize when I've fallen for this lie. I know I am attaching my happiness to what money can buy when I am feeling discontent, sorry for myself, or jealous. It happens especially when I scroll through Instagram and look at the homes other people have or fun things they can do because of their money. Those feelings are there to alert me that I'm misplacing the value of money. I'm giving it the wrong priority in my heart.

I hate to admit this, but I still struggle at times with thinking money can make me happy. Thankfully, I am now able to recognize this lie quickly, so I do not spend too long at my own pity party, but for years I had myself fooled. I never really thought of myself as someone who had such a misplaced money mindset, but there have been moments when my past actions proved otherwise.

Probably one of the most embarrassing moments I created for myself was when my husband was offered a new job with a significant salary increase. Chad had pursued a Master's degree in education and wanted to become a principal after teaching in the classroom for several years. For some reason we both went to the new school to meet with the administration and sign the contract. As we sat around the conference room table with forms spread out in front of us, I blurted out, "Honey, just sign the papers so they can show us the money." The reaction from the room full of professionals was awkward and uncomfortable. I suddenly realized my remark was very distasteful and I'm still embarrassed whenever I run into one of the gentlemen who was present that day. (I hope he doesn't remember it . . . I still do, and it's been more than twenty years!)

It might sound like it was an off the cuff remark made in jest, but really it revealed where my heart was at that time in my life. I was so excited my husband was getting a significant salary increase because it meant we would be able to afford a nicer house in a better neighborhood where we could talk long walks and the kids could ride their bikes. I thought all those things would make me happy. But all this lie does is cause us to waste energy, like a hamster on a wheel—always spinning but going nowhere, all the while feeling frustrated, discontent, and unsatisfied.

Gratitude sets my heart right again. This heart exercise of focusing on what we have instead of what we lack ushers in peace, contentment, and satisfaction. Gratitude turns what we have into enough. It is an instant attitude adjustment as it shifts my eyes from staring down at my earthly possessions to looking up, thanking my Heavenly provider. I was inspired to keep a gratitude journal after I read Ann Voskamp's book, One Thousand Gifts. She encouraged her readers to look for ordinary blessings and to write them down as a transformative spiritual discipline. She explained that "it is only in this expressing of gratitude for the life we already have, we discover the life we have always wanted, a life we can take, give thanks for and break for others." So that's what I did.

I bought a brand-new journal and jotted things down like listening to my children laugh as they splashed in the lake, having my husband's help bringing in groceries, warm blankets, and birthday texts. I looked for the simple pleasures like the smell of fresh coffee to the more significant, such as paid bills. I included my son finding a snapper turtle and the sight of red geraniums. I collected so many entries that they morphed along with the seasons. Flowers gave way to falling leaves and cozy fires on a cold winter evening. I wrote down everything I experienced, from the physical to the emotional to the spiritual. I inscribed the words Forgiveness, Mercy, Salvation, Worship, Prayer, Hope and Grace. My last entry was number 2,015, and I don't know why I stopped. Perhaps it was because I was tired, but not from journaling. Tired from allowing money to dictate my happiness when I realized through the discipline of gratitude that happiness comes in so many forms. In essence, our blessings are like sunbeams all stretching from one source—the Son.

We will always be richer than some and poorer than others, but thanking God for meeting our every need reminds us that true happiness is found in a rich relationship with God— not in anything money can buy. It's absurd and foolish to think that money will ensure a happy marriage. It simply cannot. When each spouse believes happiness is found in a rich relationship with God and not in money, we become united as a couple and take a step on the right path toward a fulfilling life and marriage.

15. Money is a Test of Our Heart

"Tell those who are rich in this world not to be proud and not to trust in their money, which will soon be gone. But their trust should be in the living God, who richly gives us all we need for our enjoyment." (1 Timothy 6:17 NLT)

The reason Jesus talks about money more than any other topic in Scripture is because money is the number one rival for God's place in our hearts. He knows money has the power to lure our heart away from God. Once we start misplacing the value of money by trusting in the dollar to meet our needs, Almighty God no longer occupies His rightful place in our lives. Jesus says essentially, "You can't love me and money, nor can you serve both of us either. You have to pick one."

It boils down to one thing: money is a heart issue. That's the real reason people don't like talking about it, myself included. It exposes the dark corners of our hearts. It reveals cobwebs spun from lies of insecurity and lack of trust in God. We think we have kept ourselves swept and clean, but when tough times hit, we are caught in a web of worry about how we are going to pay off that loan, get through Christmas, or make the next car payment. Cobwebs are terrific reminders that it is time to clean house.

It has been said, "If you want to know where your heart is, look at your bank statement." Our spending habits will reveal if we are passing or failing, as God uses money to examine four spiritual chambers in our heart:

1. Our Loyalty – We are wise to ask ourselves, "Whose interest am I serving? Mine or God's? Is my money going toward God's kingdom or my closet? God's kingdom or my hobby? God's kingdom or my man-made estate? Why is it so hard to throw fifty bucks toward the non-profit that helps the homeless or after-school programs for kids but we can drop one hundred bucks on an evening out with friends or a new pair of running shoes? Why?"

One of the hardest seats to get out of is the throne in our mini-kingdom. It is so comfortable, and it feels good when we are perched at the top, making decisions about what best serves us, what impacts our level of comfort and appearance in front of others, and what is convenient for our family without spending equal or more time deciding on how to serve God's interests.

Admittedly, our tendency is to make sure me, myself, and I are taken care of before considering the less fortunate or kingdom-building causes right in front of me. We are so completely loyal to ourselves that it feels unnatural, uncomfortable, even painful at times to release the grip of the dollar in our hand and let it rest on those in need. Money gives us the opportunity to prove our love and loyalty to the real King, who owns it all anyway.

2. Our Character – Are you one to cut corners when it comes to tithing, taxes, and other commitments you have made? That can be tempting, and if I am stepping on your toes, forgive me! We all fall short. I certainly have many times. How often have we had the opportunity to correct a clerk when given the incorrect total of a purchase? I have been known to rationalize a time or two, thinking, "Well, that is not my fault. I guess God just wanted to 'bless' me today."

What about the times when you get out to your car and notice the case of water bottles on the bottom of your shopping cart that you forgot to point out to the cashier? Do you go back into the store to pay, or load them into your backseat, rationalizing to yourself, "I spend enough money in that store. A case of water isn't going to matter." I myself am guilty.

God does give "pop quizzes" when it comes to testing our character. Whether in large amounts of tax evasion or taking supplies from work, our character is worth more than whatever amount we are trying to save. If you are making decisions with your money that are chipping away at your character, grace allows us to begin where we are and do the next right thing.

3. Our Self-Control – Forgive me for asking such a pointed question, but are you willing to live on less than what you make? Stop to consider, "Do I really need the most expensive one all the time? Do I really need twelve of the same thing?" These are tough questions, especially when you walk by a 75 percent off sale rack and you like the sweater so much that you have to have one in every color!

I will never forget the time Chad and I impulsively bought a large, flat screen television. Both of us were mesmerized by the slashed price like a couple of tourists being hypnotized by a snake charmer. After paying (probably with the store's credit card), we carried that huge box to the car, pulled out of the parking lot, and immediately fell out of our trance. We looked at each other and, without saying a word, made a U-turn, walked back to the store, and returned the item we had bought just ten minutes earlier.

The word self-control is so misleading because, I don't know about you, but my Self has no control. That is precisely the problem. When it comes to doing what is right and good, I have no control. That is why it's so important for God's Spirit to be in control. He is the only one who has the power to help us overcome any temptation we face or weakness we carry.

Consider this passage from Galatians chapter five, which explains our internal conflict so directly:

> "So I advise you to live according to your new life in the Holy Spirit. Then you won't be doing what your sinful nature craves. The old sinful nature loves to do evil which is just opposite from what the Holy Spirit wants. And the Spirit gives us desires that are opposite from what the sinful nature desires. These two forces are constantly fighting each other, and your choices are never free from this conflict . . . But when the Holy Spirit controls our lives, he will produce this kind of fruit in us: love, joy, peace, patience, kindness, goodness, faithfulness, gentleness and self-control. Here there is no conflict with the law."
>
> (Galatians 5:16-17, 22 NLT)

A friend once said, "The only thing good in me is God." I couldn't agree more and when it comes to controlling myself and my money, I can only make good choices with His help!

4. Our Love for People – Does your compassion in your heart extend all the way to the wallet in your hand, or does it stop short? Jesus taught that the most important thing is to

153

love God and love people. Our money gives us an opportunity each week to do just that through our tithe (which means ten percent). God's not after our money. He is after our heart. Joyfully giving back ten percent of our income to Him is one way we can pass the test and prove He has our heart.

God gave me a simple illustration to prove this point after I bought a pack of gum for my daughter. As she opened the pack, I asked for one piece and she flat out said no. I was upset, not because of the gum, but that she didn't value our relationship or appreciate that I bought it for her. Giving a portion back to God and sharing what we have with the people He loves proves our heart is in the right place.

There's also a flip side to this test. Not only does God use money to test the condition of our heart, He invites us to use it to test Him. In Malachi 3:10, He encourages His people to:

> "'Bring all the tithes into the storehouse so there will be enough food in my Temple. If you do,' says the Lord Almighty, 'I will open the windows of heaven for you. I will pour out a blessing so great you won't have enough room to take it in! Try it! Let me prove it to you!'"

God promises He will take care of us when we give the rightful place in our heart to Him. Are you passing the tests of loyalty, character, self-control, and love? What grade would you give yourself?

16. Money is Temporary

"Don't wear yourself out trying to get rich! Why waste your

time? For riches can disappear as though they have wings of a

bird!" (Proverbs 23:4-5 NLT)

That sounds like something a father would say, doesn't it?

Imagine Solomon and his son strolling through gorgeous

gardens having a heart-to-heart or perhaps sharing a moment

while stringing a bow or fixing an arrow. I'm not sure what a

king who has everything does with his son, but a father's heart

is unchanging through the ages. A good father, no matter his

station in life, has an intense desire to pass on knowledge to

help his son be the man he's meant to be. Most fathers want

their sons to avoid the mistakes they made and turn out to be a better man than he is. King Solomon is no exception. He does not mince words when it comes to sharing sound financial principles with his boy. His straightforward approach says that working just to accumulate as much money as you can simply to get rich is not a worthy life goal. In fact, the opposite is true; it is a waste of time.

It's quite ironic coming from the wealthiest man who ever lived—and please don't misunderstand. There is absolutely nothing wrong with being rich or making money to provide for your family, put money into retirement, have nice things, or enjoy amazing experiences. But if your motive is to gain wealth at all costs at the expense of what is really important (your family, character, and relationships) and it's your number one priority, don't bother. It's all temporary. There is nothing of lasting value there.

Even though we work hard to earn it, there are so many ways to lose it. Few things are less secure than money; investments tank, inflation rises, bills come, cars break, kids need food (go figure!), business partners steal, and fires and floods destroy. Even if we manage to keep every dime we have earned tucked safely underneath our mattress, there will come a time when money won't serve a purpose. We will eventually reach a point where we do not need it anymore. It will be of no use to us, because we will be gone!

You've probably heard it said, "You can't take it with you," and it's true. No one has ever seen a hearse pulling a U-Haul. This was our experience as we sat with Chad's grandfather in his final moments on earth. We gathered with a few family members in the small, sparse room at his nursing home. I remember looking around at the bare paneled walls, my eyes landing on his gold wristwatch. I thought to myself, "This is all he has left, and what good is it doing him now?" His kids sold his house, his car, all his earthly possessions, and any dime left in his bank account did not matter anymore. All of it was gone. The only thing of value was the intangible legacy of what he was leaving behind—his three kids, his grandchildren, and the lives he touched along the way.

There are certain moments in life that give pause to what really matters, and certainly death is one of them. That day, this truth sunk deep in my heart like a heavy rock heaved into a murky lake: Money is temporary and possessions don't matter, but people do. In the grand scheme of things, my kitchen size doesn't matter. My clothing label doesn't matter, nor does the make and model of my vehicle. All of these are temporary and meaningless in the long run. When all is said and done, I guarantee we won't regret how we spent, invested, and gave in ways that pointed others to God.

One of the most eye-opening experiences I had in learning this truth about money was when I worked at a tax and accounting office. A family member owned her own firm and needed someone during tax season to man the front desk. She asked if I would be interested in the part-time position, as she needed a friendly face to put people at ease. Let's be honest, no one enjoys getting their taxes done, so she figured a warm smile might be good for business and make the chore at least tolerable. I assured her I knew absolutely zero about numbers and still use my fingers to add. My dad and brother were the accountants in the family; I was more of a word girl. But she assured me that she would teach me everything I needed to know, so I took the job.

The part I most enjoyed was talking to the different people who came into the office (surprise). I thought I was the type of person who treated everyone with the same level of respect and courtesy, but when I started seeing their financial records, I'm ashamed to say my attitude toward some changed. I was shocked to see an older man dressed in dirty jeans and a raggedy wool jacket wearing a faded hat hand me papers that said his net worth was in the millions. I was equally shocked when I'd see someone pull up in a brand new, expensive car and I'd notice their name brand clothes or purse, but then when I opened their file to see their income, I'd wonder how they could afford what they were driving or wearing.

I saw couples living on meager wages give half of their income away to charities and good causes, and I noticed that a few very wealthy people hoarded every dime they owned. My takeaway from that job was that appearances are just that— appearances. What we see on the outside about a person does not reveal their whole story, yet we make permanent judgments based on something so temporary, like money.

People are people. Our pastor has a saying, "The problem with most of us is we are just like the rest of us." We are all the same on the inside. Each person on this planet was masterfully designed and created by God Himself, who has a purpose for us and longs for us to be in relationship with Him. That's it. So why do we spend so much time chasing after and judging by externals that have no eternal value?

Money is of this earth and will pass away. People are the only things that we take with us into eternity! Instead of spending so much time working toward riches or the temporary social status that comes from money, let us spend our time investing in what has eternal value—the people God has placed around us. Jesus says money is not a true source of happiness, it is a test of our heart and only temporary. To God, money is really just a tool we are to use to point people to a relationship with Him.

17. Money is a Tool

"Tell them to use their money to do good. They should be rich in good works and should give generously to those in need, always being ready to share with others whatever God has given them."

(1 Timothy 6:18 NLT)

Money is like a hammer—a tool that can build something up or tear it down. It can be used for good work or bad. We are encouraged to use it in ways that meet the needs of people and further build God's kingdom. When we put our money into causes that introduce others to God or move people one step closer in their relationship with Him, we are using it wisely and valuing it properly. Money is just a tool to help people. And one more thing: we are told not to be stingy with it, either!

Generosity is a mark of a true Jesus follower. While speaking to a group of people, Jesus remarks that the godly are generous givers and that we can't out-give God. He says:

> "If you give, you will receive. Your gift will return to you in full measure, pressed down, shaken together to make room for more, and running over. Whatever measure you use in giving – large or small – it will be used to measure what is given back to you." (Luke 6:38 NLT)

Chad and I have found that if we take care of God's business, He takes care of ours. You probably know what I'm talking about. We've all tasted that sweet satisfaction that comes from helping someone. I have a friend who is a single mom and needed work done on her house. Chad and I bought a bunch of supplies and went over one weekend. I helped paint her living room while Chad raised the deck so it wouldn't collapse. After we completed the projects, she was thrilled, and we felt good! We don't give to get, but generosity is like a boomerang—it doesn't leave our hand and never returns. What we give out always comes back in the form of another blessing. We simply can't out-give God. The Old Testament and New Testament lists the benefits of generosity like a commercial for a prescription medicine, only without negative side effects:

Generosity honors God – "Whoever is generous to the needy honors God." (Proverbs 14:31)

Generosity draws us toward God – "For where your treasure is, there your heart will be also." (Matthew 6:21)

Generosity demonstrates our faith in God – "I pray that your partnership with us in the faith may be effective in deepening your understanding of every good thing we share for the sake of Christ." (Philemon 1:6)

Generosity brings God's blessing – "Generous people will be blessed." (Proverbs 22:9)

Generosity increases our happiness – "In everything they did, I showed you that by this kind of hard work we must help the weak, remembering the words the Lord

Jesus himself said, 'it is more blessed to give than to receive.'" (Acts 20:35)

Generosity multiplies my money – "A generous person will prosper; whoever refreshes others will be refreshed." (Proverbs 11:25)

Generosity brings God's protection – "Good will come to those who are generous and lend freely, who conduct their affairs with justice. Surely the righteous will never be shaken; they will be remembered forever." (Psalm 112:5-6)

The Biggest Benefit of All

". . . by doing this they will be storing up their treasure as a good foundation for the future so they may take hold of real life." (1 Timothy 6:19 NLT)

In all of Jesus's teaching about money, He tries to get us to connect our earthly priorities with an eternal perspective. He reminds us not to be so concerned with the here and now, but to rather focus on the hereafter. Real life comes after this life! It's easy to lose this perspective when the kids need braces, your car breaks down, college loans are due, and you're scraping just to get groceries for the week, because money affects us in the here and now. But it makes a big difference when both partners value money the way Jesus taught, that:

- It's not a true source of happiness, and it's absurd to think otherwise

- It's simply a test to examine if God occupies the right place in our heart

- It's only temporary; working hard for the sake of simply accumulating wealth and possessions is a waste of time

Money is just a tool. We are to use whatever amount we've been given as our tool to build His kingdom and meet the needs of others. Only then can we unite, not fight, and position ourselves to fulfill God's purpose as a couple.

18. Plan Together

What comes to your mind when you hear the words "financial plan" or "budget?" Some of us start to squirm, because what we really heard was "restriction." In my days of credit card spending, the mention of the word "budget" practically gave me hives. I was fearful that I would have to ask for a dollar to buy a candy bar and I did not want to be held accountable for my spending habits.

It was not until Chad and I completed a class on learning sound financial principles that I understood that a financial plan can really bring a wealth of comfort, joy, and freedom into your relationship. A budget is the most practical way to prioritize your money and keep you united over the topic. Trust me, I know it can be scary in the beginning, but it is a very wise and freeing thing to do. Turning again to Solomon's wisdom:

"Know the state of your flocks." (Proverbs 27:23 NLT)

Or in modern terms, know the state of your finances.

"My child, don't lose sight of good planning and insight. Hang on to them, for they fill you with life and bring you honor and respect. They keep you safe on your way and keep your feet from stumbling. You can lie down without fear and enjoy pleasant dreams. You need not be afraid of disaster or the destruction that comes upon the wicked, for the LORD is your security." (Proverbs 3:21 NLT)

A Financial Plan Rids Anxiety and Allows for

Availability

Planning is critical. Adhering to the plan is crucial. Maybe at times a little painful, but in the end, there is peace on so many levels. A financial plan is more than just sticking to a budget, more than reducing debt, more than saving for retirement. You are ridding yourself and your marriage of much unwanted frustration, anxiety, and conflict that has a domino effect in all areas. Once Chad and I gave ourselves permission for an "adult allowance" that we could freely spend on what we wanted, I stopped hiding bags in my trunk until Chad left for work. It felt good to stop keeping secrets. Secrets can silently kill a marriage.

Putting a pen to paper will help you reevaluate your priorities. You may find that you don't need to spend so many hours at the office, or perhaps you'll be able to get rid of that second job. Maybe you'll discover the goal you have been pursuing is no longer where your heart is because God has revealed different plans that include your spouse.

It has taken us years to discover our strengths and passions, and to learn how God has wired us to complement each other. God made Chad a leader, and with my "gift of gab" we make a great team when it comes to sharing our experiences and helping and teaching others in group settings. We now work in more ministry-related capacities, and we never would have dreamed we'd be doing this ten, even five, years ago. But looking back, we can see how God nudged us to get our finances in order so we could be ready when He called!

We want to position ourselves so we can say "YES!" when God calls. It is unlikely He will give a two-week notice when He presents us with a kingdom-building opportunity. We cannot find a single scenario in Scripture where God showed up, whether it was to Abraham, Moses, Jonah, or Peter, and said, "I have this opportunity for you, and I'll be back later to tell you all about it." No, He said to each of them, "Now is the time. Let's go." Do you really want to tell God, "Sorry, I'm too overwhelmed at work, I really can't. Now is just not a good time." Or "Sorry, we don't have the money to help."

A financial plan will help unite and allow you to say YES to God's purpose for your marriage. Good theories always look better on paper. Implementing ideas can be tricky, so here are three suggestions to make planning together go smoothly and feel less overwhelming:

1. Common Goal

What is it that you want to accomplish? What goal or purpose are you working toward? It's profitable to think short-term and long-term. When Chad and I felt called to help build marriages, we realized this required more of us than we could devote while working full-time. We had to rework our finances so one of us could quit our job. Perhaps you'd like to pay off a car so you can give to a specific ministry that's close to your heart. Maybe your desire is to save for a family mission trip or start a business together. It's important to center your planning and prioritizing on a common goal, which will also require Step Two.

2. Clear Communication

In the world of real estate, the financial experts say, "Location, Location, Location!" But when it comes to communication, relational experts cry, "Timing! Timing! Timing!" Timing is everything. Money is an important—and sometimes difficult—subject to discuss and we know it can lead to heated arguments. A budget or anything money-related isn't something I bring up during the fourth quarter of the Lions football game, nor does Chad choose to chat about it when I'm on my way out the door to go shopping with my girls. We have learned it is best to schedule a time and place and call it safe. You can get through anything if you know it is only going to take thirty minutes, and if an argument starts to arise, close the books, and walk away. Take time to pray and decide to come back again later.

3. Compromise

Remember, unity doesn't mean uniformity. We are called to one purpose, but we are still two unique people, so unity requires compromise. You and your spouse will have to be intentional in keeping an attitude of give and take. Hypothetically, if our plan is to reduce debt, then I might have to give up my Kohl's credit card and my husband may have to relinquish his Cabela's card. Or I might commit to saying, "I won't buy any more expensive soap" and he'll agree not to buy top-of-the-line shotgun shells. If your plan is to save for a mission trip, the compromise might be, "I'll work extra hours and you pick up the slack at home."

Your plan is going to be as unique as your relationship. What works for Chad and me is not going to be the same as what works for your marriage. Each of our situations are different, but God's purpose for us is the same: to use our money as a tool to build up His kingdom and meet the needs of others in our own unique way. Whatever that looks like is for you and your spouse to decide. Share your passions and dreams and watch God's plan unfold. He'll show you the way as you do the next thing!

Regardless of whether you are rich or poor, a plan that prioritizes money according to God's values will create unity in our marriage and allow us to fulfill His purpose for us as a couple; it's the only way to a secure future and to enjoy a rewarding marriage that money can't buy!

We become united over money when each spouse values money the way Jesus taught. Planning together will position us to fulfill God's plan for our marriage and money.

Questions to Consider:

1. Can you relate to one of the fictional couples in what could be real-life scenarios? Explain.

2. Which one of the four money values do you struggle with most and why?

3. Complete the sentence: If money were no object, I would . . .

Notes:

IV.

To Love and to Cherish

Deepening Intimacy

Intimacy is deepened when I cherish the physical, emotional, and spiritual aspects of my spouse equally.

19. A Tension to Manage

For many couples, intimacy is a subject handled much like a hot potato. They can hold it for a few seconds, maybe toss it around for a little bit, but then set it down because it is just too hot to touch. Why is that? Why do we dance around, avoid it, and squirm like a bunch of middle school kids in health class when the topic comes up?

Much of our perception about intimacy is formed naturally by how we were raised. I grew up in a home where we did not talk about things like intimacy (which I thought was the nice word Christians used for sex). I didn't see my parents hug and kiss very much except when my dad was heading off to work, nor do I ever remember hearing about it in church other than that we were told, "Don't have sex until you're married." My idea was developed by what I learned from kids at school and what I saw on movies (very accurate sources, I might add). Since I was left to use my imagination and wasn't sure what was true, I felt uncomfortable talking about the topic in front of people and, at times, even with my husband.

Chad's parents, on the other hand, were very affectionate with each other. He remembers having friends come over only to be embarrassed because his parents would be making out in the kitchen! That was normal at their house. When we got married, I was totally uncomfortable holding hands in public, much less kissing in front of our kids. I thought all of that had to take place after 10:00 p.m. with the lights off! Chad thought that was odd and could not understand why I felt that way.

Our ideas of intimacy are as different as our personalities and experiences. We have talked to couples who have been hurt in a past relationship or by their spouse, so intimacy is a very tender topic. It takes a lot of time and effort for people who have been wounded, abused, or betrayed to heal and risk being vulnerable again, so intimacy can be a very painful discussion.

For others, intimacy is something they are too tired for, so they simply avoid it. Admittedly, life throws significant challenges at times that decrease our capacity to enjoy true intimacy, whether it is a health issue, a stressful job, or extended family crisis. Even our own kids can steal so much of our time and energy to the point that we just cannot even "go there."

I think back to my days of nursing babies who were constantly attached to me (literally!) and felt if one more person so much as touched me that day, I would in some way hurt them. And then I'd flop into bed, praying for a few hours of uninterrupted sleep and all of a sudden, I'd feel my husband's hand sliding under the covers, and I'd think, "No, no, no . . . I can'ttttt . . . please just go to sleep!"

While our experiences, situations, and perceptions are all different, take a minute to own yours. What do you think of when you hear the word intimacy? What particular word or feeling pops into your mind? Sexual, exciting, disappointing, painful, personal, physical, anxious, adventurous, dirty, desirable, enjoyable, longing, frustrating, emotional, confusing? Perhaps all fit your definition or maybe none, yet in order to experience intimacy fully, our head needs to understand what we are capable of and what our entire being— spirit, soul, and body—is designed for. There has to be more to intimacy than just hot sex. To gather more information, we will turn to the first page of Scripture and piece together what complete, true, pure, God-designed intimacy is.

What God Had in Mind

Scripture opens in Genesis with the creation story; let's pick up at the point where Adam is standing alone in the Garden of Eden. He notices all of the animals are in pairs; each has a partner, but for some reason, Adam does not. Little did he know that the best was yet to come! The creation drama was coming to a climax as God supernaturally anesthetized Adam into a deep sleep. Judging by Adam's gasp-filled reaction upon waking, God's plan turned out to be exciting and surprisingly satisfying.

"The Lord God made a woman from the rib and brought her to Adam. 'At last!' Adam exclaimed. 'She is part of my own flesh and bone! She will be called 'woman' because she

was taken out of man.' This explains why a man leaves his father and mother and is joined to his wife and the two are united into one. Now although Adam and his wife were both naked, neither of them felt any shame.' (Genesis 2:24-25 NLT, emphasis added)

It can be tempting to skim over these short, perhaps familiar verses. At first glance, what may seem like minor details actually give major clues to help frame a picture of what complete intimacy looks like. Notice it says they were "naked and neither of them felt any shame." Adam and Eve were totally transparent with each other and they had nothing to hide from each other. They were naked physically and felt confident and unembarrassed in their own skin. They were connected emotionally since there were no distractions, past hurts, harsh words, or other relational ties between them causing shame. And if we fast forward a few verses, we see the third aspect:

"Toward evening they heard the LORD God walking about in the garden . . ." (Genesis 3:8).

They were bonded spiritually by sharing an honest relationship with God.

Adam and Eve were not alone in the garden; Creator God was actively engaged in their daily life. He was completely involved and interacted with the first couple, so talking to God was a normal part of their everyday routine. I wish Scripture provided more details. My imagination wonders, would they be sitting under an apple tree and, boom, God just appeared? I don't know, but what is clear is that God was present. By putting the physical, emotional, and spiritual pieces together, we grasp a better understanding of God's original design, from which we can define intimacy as:

A totally transparent and deeply fulfilling connection that includes all three aspects of our human nature—

the physical, emotional, and spiritual.

Picture a three-legged stool. To function properly, all three legs need to be in place and balanced. If one leg is wobbly, broken, or missing, you will not have a sturdy stool to sit on. In the same way, intimacy has three parts—the emotional, physical, and spiritual—and all three are of equal value and importance. When they come together we experience complete intimacy—a mutually satisfying and deeply fulfilling connection of oneness.

Without understanding this trifecta and only focusing on one leg of the stool by saying things like, "I wish we had sex more often," or "I wish I could talk to my spouse and not feel anxious," or "It would be nice if we were on the same page spiritually," we are missing the big idea. The key to oneness is understanding that each aspect is not mutually exclusive of the others, but dependent upon each other. All three aspects work together to create complete intimacy. So, while there may be issues that need to be addressed in each area, intimacy is not a problem to solve but a tension to manage. Intimacy on the deepest, truest level is achieved when we give each other an all-access pass to every part of us—the physical, emotional, and spiritual.

What Do You See When You Look into Me?

In another sense, intimacy is an answer to the question that lies deep within our heart and is revealed when we break down the pronunciation of the word, "in-to-me-see." Our heart is asking, "When you look into me, what do you see? Do you see anything of value? Do you see me as someone worthy of your time and energy? Do you want to experience a deep and satisfying connection with me?"

We essentially answered "yes" to that question when we chose to marry. Our vows include "to love and to cherish" because we looked at another person and recognized their worth. We saw our spouse as someone who possessed tremendous value, a person we wanted to experience complete intimacy with, so we promised to treat them—to love and cherish them—as the treasure they are for the rest of our lives. Solomon has a beautifully poetic way of expressing his cherishing heart:

"You have ravished my heart, my treasure, my bride. I am overcome by one glance of your eyes, by a single bead of your necklace. How sweet is your love, my treasure, my bride! How much better it is than wine!" (Song of Solomon 4:9-10a NLT)

Our marriage journey began with a general under-standing of the vow, "to love and to cherish," but how many of us knew it was the key to experiencing the depths of intimacy? (For those who thought this was just going to be about sex, stick with me. I think you will be pleased in the end.)

We Cherish What is Important

Shortly after I moved out, my parents were victims of a house fire started by a compact disc lying on an upstairs bedroom floor. It was mid-summer when the sun came through the window and heated the carpet to such a degree that it ignited a spark, and fire spread to the other rooms. My mom was in the kitchen on the main floor when she noticed smoke billowing from the upstairs window and yelled for everyone to get out of the house. She quickly grabbed their golden retriever and ran outside. Thankfully, no one was injured but the entire house suffered damage.

Heaven forbid, but if your house were on fire, what is something you would grab before you ran outside? Most likely, like my mom, you would scoop up your kids and pets and if time allowed, perhaps some memorable pictures, jewelry, or essential documents. Whatever you snatched, it would be important and something you cherished.

Cherish isn't a word we use every day, but when we do, it's attached to something of value: "I cherish those times I spent with my dad now that he's gone," or "I cherish my grandmother's Bible." To cherish something means we value it. Paul, a New Testament writer, points to something all of us cherish—our own bodies.

Ephesians 5:28 NLT says, "... husbands ought to love their wives as they <u>love their own bodies.</u> For a man is actually loving himself when he loves his wife. No one hates his own body but nourishes and cherishes it just as Christ does the church."

Paul is stating the obvious: we humans have a natural tendency to value our own body without giving it much thought. Every day we nurture it with food and water, protect it by wearing clothes while taking precautions to avoid germs. We give it attention as we work out and try to stay healthy because it is a priority to us. We cherish our bodies in the same way a man cherishes an expensive sports car. He is not going to leave it outside with the keys in it! No, he is going to pay careful attention to it and protect it, and he is also going to show it off! That's how we treat something we cherish . . . but what does it mean to cherish someone?

To Love and To Cherish

What exactly did we promise when we spoke those vows? We all know about love—isn't that the reason we got married in the first place? Even if we thought love was primarily a feeling, we knew it involved some level of sacrifice and commitment. But what about the word cherish? To be honest, I did not give it much thought on my wedding day, but in my vows I promised to love and to cherish my husband. Was I promising to never let the warm fuzzies I had in the beginning get cold? Was I making a vow to treat him like a king and in return he was supposed to treat me as his queen? How exactly does this play out in ordinary, everyday life?

Believe it or not, "to love and to cherish" are not feelings that come and go, nor are these outdated and antiquated vows that no longer apply. They are relevant actions that, if practiced, have the power to take our marriage to new levels of intimacy where we experience deeper levels of joy, satisfaction, and contentment we didn't even know existed.

Growing up in the Great Lakes State, I have been around large bodies of water my entire life. I am a fairly good swimmer and have spent many summers splashing in the waves of Lake Michigan. As beautiful as our freshwater lake is, it is not filled with swarms of colorful fish or coral reefs, so imagine my surprise when I signed up for a snorkeling excursion while visiting the Bahamas.

I was eager for my underwater adventure and, upon jumping in, realized there was more than meets the eye. As I swam away from the boat, I was mesmerized by the sparkling blue surface and thought it was truly breathtaking. That view alone was worth the dive, but then I put my mask on and peered further under the surface. My eyes grew wide as schools of brightly colored fish of all shapes and sizes skimmed across my shins. I did not notice them while on the boat, but there they were, waiting to surprise me under the ripples. And then, after the fish passed and the water settled, I began to explore and something a little deeper caught my attention. I could see sand swirling in circles just above the ocean floor, so I took a deep breath and dove down. Gliding way below, a group of massive manta rays dragged their bellies across the sandy bottom. I froze, captivated by their size and beauty as they floated by effortlessly.

If you can stretch your imagination with me, I liken this experience to loving and cherishing. Love is the excitement I had when I jumped in the water and was eager for the adventure to begin. Cherish is drawing those big breaths and going deeper to experience the beauty, joy, and satisfaction below the surface that I didn't know existed previously. I would still have had a fun time swimming around near the top, but taking action to experience what was underneath made it spectacular.

Other ways to understand how "love and cherish" go hand-in-hand can be formed by observing a professional dance couple glide across a ballroom floor in perfect time, or by watching a pair ride in sync on a tandem bicycle. The two do not compete but complement each other, much like love is the nurturing aspect of marriage while cherishing adds the exciting parts. Gary Thomas, in his book, Cherish, explains that most wives do not want their husbands to "love" them in the sense of just being committed; they want to feel special. And most men want their wives to not only love them, but "like" them—that makes them feel valued.

Love and cherish go together like peas and carrots, and each are individually talked about in Scripture. Love is woven throughout the entire Bible but especially highlighted in 1 Corinthians 13, while cherish has its own book entirely—the Song of Solomon. The book is extremely passionate and describes the physical component of marriage, proving that God created passion and sex to be enjoyed and nurtured as part of the complete intimacy experience. Let's look further at how each are described as Gary Thomas compares the two:

Love is about being altruistic and selfless – "Love is patient and kind." (1 Corinthians 13:4 NLT)

Cherish is about passion and excitement – "Kiss me again and again, for your love is sweeter than wine." (Song of Solomon 1:2 NLT)

Love tends to be quiet and understated – "Love does not envy; it does not boast." (1 Corinthians 13:4 NIV)

Cherish is bold and vivacious – "My lover is dark and dazzling, better than 10,000 others!" (Song of Solomon 5:10 NLT)

Love puts up with a lot as it "always hopes, always perseveres." (1 Corinthians 13:7 NIV)

Cherish enjoys a lot: "His mouth is altogether sweet; he is lovely in every way." (Song of Solomon 5:16 NLT)

Love is about commitment – "Love endures all things." (1 Corinthians 13:7 ESV)

Cherish is about appreciation – "Arise my beloved, my fair one, and come away . . . let me see you, let me hear your voice. For your voice is pleasant and you are lovely." (Song of Solomon 2:13-14 NLT)

Gary Thomas goes on to say that comparing the two doesn't diminish one over the other, but highlights how they complement each other. "Love is the strength of the relationship, and cherish gives it the sparkle! Cherish polishes love to make our marriage shine." Honestly, I do not know why we talk so much about love and so little about cherish. Maybe we see them as one and the same, but clearly, they are different.

When it comes to deepening intimacy, cherishing is the secret weapon, but knowing this is not sufficient; we must be intentional to experience the difference. It is not enough to just sit around in a rocking chair knowing you have to lose twenty pounds. You gotta get up and take action! It is the principle, information plus application equals transformation that applies to loving and cherishing in our marriage. We are always one action away from deeper intimacy. So, what are some practical ways we can cherish our spouse? Let's find out together.

20. Attention

When we give our full attention, we are treating our spouse as our #1 priority and making them feel like they are the most important person in the world!

"There may be 60 wives, all queens, and 80 concubines and unnumbered virgins available to me. But I would still choose my dove, my perfect one." (Song of Solomon 6:8 NLT, emphasis added)

Of the numberless women available to Solomon, there was only one woman who had his full attention, which had to make her feel pretty special. Cherished. I am glad I do not have to compete with sixty other wives and eighty concubines and an unnumbered quantity of virgins! I'm pretty sure my husband could not handle all of that estrogen anyway. But on

August 10th, 1991, he did pick me! On a college campus of over 5,000 people, I was the one he thought about as he laid on the bottom bunk in his dorm room. Being chosen is a wonderful feeling that makes us feel wanted, accepted, desired, and special. Ideally, this isn't something that fades over time. Every time we make our spouse feel like they are our number one, we are communicating that they are valued, and they feel cherished.

Remember how you felt when you first saw your spouse on your wedding day? Maybe you can't remember that far back. It has been thirty years for us, so my memory is a little fuzzy. More recently I think of watching our son, Alex, on his wedding day bawl like a baby while Hannah, moments away from becoming his wife, walks down the aisle. No one else in the world mattered more to him in that moment than she did. Everyone in attendance faded into the background as his eyes locked on his chosen bride. She had his full attention, and his emotional reaction was so heartwarming that I do not think there was a dry eye in the entire place! While Alex was crying tears of joy, Hannah's smile was radiant, knowing that her man was "all eyes on her."

The good news is we do not have to let this dynamic be a once-in-a-lifetime experience—this can be our everyday reality. We might not be overcome with such emotion every time our spouse walks through the door, but when we turn down the clamor of everyday noise, turn away from the competition of other men and women, and turn our eyes toward our spouse, we are communicating to them that they are the most important person in the world, making our spouse feel cherished.

Let's put ourselves in Adam and Eve's shoes for a minute (if they even had shoes). How would you treat your spouse if the two of you were all alone in a perfect paradise where the only distractions were animals and God who walked about in the cool of the day? The first couple did not have the interruptions of social media, a TV blaring in the background as they cooked dinner, work emails, text messages, Snapchat notifications, Google calendars to update, or appointments to schedule. They did not have to worry about any of that technology that steals so much of our time and attention. Talk about the perfect situation to be emotionally connected! They had plenty of time to give each other their full attention in a perfect environment.

It almost sounds too obvious, but in our world of constant interruptions and distractions, giving our spouse our full attention is critically important. This means when your spouse is talking, you stop scrolling, put down your phone, and actually look at them—like, face to face. In today's culture, we are so dependent upon and fascinated by the device in our hands, we can easily ignore our loved ones in the same room— and for hours on end! Many spouses have their faces turned away looking at Facebook, Instagram, Pinterest, playing games or ... they are looking at porn.

Do you know one of the many dangers of porn is that it actually rewires the brain? It's terribly damaging and dangerous. Nothing good comes from it. And while this topic deserves its own space, more than we can give here, please consider this warning: if you are dabbling in it or have a full-blown addiction, please seek help and get out! Simply put, staring at porn is the opposite of cherishing your spouse.

Your attention is so crucial when it comes to cherishing each other that psychologists believe the simple act of making eye contact leads to deeper emotional connection. One study suggested that you could make an absolute stranger fall in love by staring into their eyes for two minutes. Whether that has actually been proven, there is a physiological basis for such a dramatic claim. Eye contact stimulates the brain to produce a chemical called phenylethylamine which causes feelings of arousal that strengthens our emotional bond. My logical train of thought says, "more eye contact = more release of the chemical = deeper bond = more intimacy." I am not a doctor, but who knew something as simple as facing your husband or wife and making eye contact when they are talking is psychologically powerful, yet also an intimate way to cherish them?

You may be thinking, "I am doing fairly well here. I do not have a problem with porn, and I do my best not to stare at my phone when my partner is talking. I honor my vows and feel like I treat my spouse well." Good for you! But may I challenge you a little bit here? Even though you are checking all of those boxes, would your spouse say they feel special? Does he or she believe they are your number one priority? Do they say they really have your full attention most of the time? Bottom line, their perception is their reality, not yours. No finger pointing here, but it is easy to coast and think because we are not doing anything particularly "wrong" we are alright—yet there is a difference in feeling cherished and feeling comfortable.

From Comfortable to Comparison

Who doesn't love being comfortable? We pretty much order our entire lives around our comfort, don't we? I prefer stretchy pants over tight jeans. We buy pillow soft mattress toppers and cars with heated seats, and we wouldn't think of buying a house without a dishwasher! There's nothing wrong with pursuing physical comfort per se, but the danger with a comfortable relationship is that it has the potential to become routine.

And *routine* can lead us into a *rut*.

And a *rut* can lead to *boredom*.

And *boredom* can lead to *comparison*.

When we are too comfortable in our marriage, there is more of a tendency to compare rather than cherish because we lose sight of what makes our spouse unique. I was attracted to Chad because of his strong personality. I admired him for his ability to have tough conversations—the type that would make my stomach nervous for a week! I admired his strength in difficult situations and his capacity to problem solve where I would be tempted to curl up into a fetal position. We are very opposite in our emotional wiring and, as much as I was attracted to his strength, he was attracted to my sensitivity. Together we make a "velvet hammer"—we are able to be both strong and soft, balancing truth and love. It is what makes our relationship unique.

Temptation accompanies comfortability when we stop appreciating each other's strengths and start taking them for granted. Our natural turns into normal and it becomes our status quo. We no longer appreciate the other person like we used to because we are just too comfortable. No one wants to move from being comfortable until something—or someone—happens. An endearing quality in someone else awakens us from our sleepy status quo and we take notice of their charming trait. Our attention has turned, and out of nowhere our appreciation for our spouse, what caught our interest in the first place, is suddenly replaced with annoyance.

Back to the Garden we go. In that distraction-free environment, Adam's attention was on Eve, and Eve's attention was on Adam. There was no one else around to compare each other to. Eve was not looking at the guy on TV, and Adam's eyes weren't wandering over to the woman in the next office cubicle. There was no one else around who was prettier, skinnier, taller, stronger, smarter, funnier, richer, or better. Eve was the standard of beauty to Adam and Adam was the standard of masculinity to Eve.

If you want to cherish your spouse, you must see them as the standard for you and not compare them to Suzy Q or Joe Schmoe. Take ownership and take interest. Declare in your mind, will, and emotions like King Solomon, "I am my beloved's, and my beloved is mine . . ." (Song of Solomon 6:3).

When you determine your spouse is the standard of beauty or masculinity, you are pronouncing that there is no one better. No one else for me! This is the ONE who has my attention and I will do my best to cherish them for their uniqueness by not comparing them to anyone else.

From Comparing to Investing

Let's pause for a quick inventory. When was the last time staring at your phone brought you joy? I know. Time you enjoy wasting is not wasted time. I like scrolling through Instagram and looking at beautifully decorated farmhouses, and Chad enjoys checking out duck hunting sites. My point here: Is your phone bringing you closer intimacy with your spouse, or causing you to drift farther apart? Is it strengthening your emotional, physical, and spiritual connection or making you feel more bored and comfortable? Again, I am not talking about all of the necessary and good uses here; I'm talking about random, pointless, mindless, time-wasting scrolling that steals our attention and certainly does not make our spouse feel important at that moment.

When was the last time comparing your spouse to someone else strengthened your relationship? When did looking at Suzy Q's legs or dreaming about Joe Schmoe's sense of humor bring you closer to your spouse? Our attention can only be in one place. If it is on someone other than our spouse, we are not giving our partner proper consideration or cherishing them as they deserve.

Here's an idea: instead of staring and comparing, we can begin cherishing by investing. Invest in what interests your spouse. Find out what makes them tick. What is a passionate topic they love discussing? What particular activity do they enjoy? Our friends Dave and Peggy are great examples of a couple who are intentional about investing in each other. Peggy is a massage therapist and the ironic thing about Dave is that he does not like back rubs! Also, Peggy is an avid outdoor and exercise enthusiast who enjoys running, yoga, biking, CrossFit, and anything that involves movement. Dave, not so much. But they respect each other's differences and will take time to do what the other person enjoys. When Peggy kayaks, Dave gets on his paddle board because he doesn't like sitting. When she wants to go biking, he'll go if she slows the pace. Dave doesn't attend Peggy's yoga classes, but it's evident he does his best to take interest in what Peggy likes. In spite of the fact he doesn't particularly enjoy these activities, his participation speaks volumes on how much he cherishes his darling wife.

If you want to show your spouse that you cherish them, give them your full attention. Put down your phone and face them. Even if you do not find what they have to say particularly interesting, you just might discover something new that will propel you toward deeper connection. When you give your spouse your full attention, it shows that you cherish them and makes them feel like your number one priority—the most important person in the world!

21. Protection

One of Chad's hunting mottos is, "There's no such thing as bad weather, just bad gear." It may or may not be true, but that is the reason he gave when Amazon delivered an expensive jacket that promised to keep him warm in negative 30-degree weather. It would be insane to sit in a field unprotected from those frigid temperatures, right? While I like to give him a hard time, I will admit his mindset points to another way we cherish our body—we protect it.

We take precautions, not only against cold weather, but also against diseases that threaten to attack our health. In the same way, we need to protect our marriage from relational germs (unhealthy behaviors and people) that can attack. It is dangerous to assume that having a "good marriage" shelters us from unwanted intruders and temptations. Protecting our spouse in strategic ways shows we cherish them.

We Must Protect Our Spouse's Reputation

Chad and I got married at ages 21 and 19. By today's standards, that is quite young. I did not have a clue about life or marriage. I lived according to my own selfish desires but found out rather quickly that did not work so well in marriage. My self-centered attitude and behaviors led to huge fights and petty arguments. I would then run to my mom in a huff and complain about my husband. I knew she liked and even loved him, but after a while I realized I was telling her all the negative stuff and leaving out the positive things he would say and do or how we solved the problem. Then one day it dawned on me: I was painting an inaccurate picture of our relationship and more importantly the type of person my husband was. I was essentially damaging his reputation in her eyes. That was not right or fair on my part, but sadly it was easy to do.

A cherishing spouse does the opposite. They stop speaking negatively and instead start talking positively. What's more, they look for opportunities to show off their spouse's positive qualities in public.

> *Song of Solomon 2:3 NLT says, "My lover is like the finest apple tree in the orchard. I am seated in his delightful shade and his fruit is delicious to eat. He brings me to the banquet hall, so everyone can see how much he loves me . . . oh feed me with your love."*

In this passage, the young man cherishes his bride by letting others see her in the best possible light. According to her response, feed me with your love, it deepened their intimacy. She wanted to be with him and experience even deeper intimacy.

Reflect on your own experience. How do you feel when your spouse compliments you in public? Picture yourselves at a dinner party and your spouse starts telling everyone about what a great spouse you are. He says, "My wife is way out of my league. I hit a home run when she said yes!" Husbands, maybe you overhear your wife say to her friends, "My husband takes such good care of me. He knows when to take the kids so I can have time to myself." Is your heart pulled favorably towards them like two lovers sharing the same spaghetti noodle? If this happened more often, how do you think it would affect your intimacy level both emotionally and physically?

We Must Protect Our Spouse's Sexuality

In the book, Cherish, Mr. Thomas concludes that "Sexually neglected or sexually unpursued men and women rarely feel cherished."

He writes, "Many men think cherish is something wives want, and they feel like less of a man even using that word. So I learned to ask my question in a different way: 'What does your wife do that makes you feel special? Honored? Noticed?' And the most typical response was, 'Well, do you want the PG answer or the real answer?'

I know this will sound cliché, but for a large percentage of men, if they're not noticed between the sheets, everything that happens outside of the bedroom is negated. I'd say this is particularly true when a husband is in his twenties, thirties, and forties. A wife usually can't underestimate the vulnerability of a man in that season of life and how he feels toward sex. As a pastor, I often encounter younger husbands, and I'm reminded of the near-daily assault many men feel trying to live lives of integrity in a pornographic world.

Women, it may help to think of your husband's sexual desires as a request to be honored. Many men work so hard, not just to contribute to the family budget, but to be true to their marital vows. There are plenty of spiritual and physical forces trying to inject compromise into your man's soul. Your physical affection is a way of honoring his commitment, his battle, and his physical desires. The husbands I talked to who felt most cherished by their wives – most honored – felt spoiled in the sexual department . . .

In the same way that a woman wants to be noticed and taken seriously when she speaks, enters a room, calls her husband, and doesn't want him looking at his smartphone while he's supposed to be talking to her, so husbands want to be noticed in the dark.

Your husband probably doesn't use this language, but he feels dishonored when you want to do a hundred different tasks besides making love. When your husband is younger and feels like he's taking second place to the children and when the frequency of intimacy is placed far behind laundry and only slightly ahead of cleaning the gutters, it's like when you're talking to your husband and you suddenly realize he hasn't heard a single word of what you've been saying."

This goes both ways as there are women whose sexual needs are higher than their husbands. To be perfectly clear, we are not licensed counselors or sex therapists. However, what we do know is we would be remiss if we did not stress the importance of the physical aspect of intimacy. There are a lot of barriers and baggage that encompass the sexual component of intimacy and there is a plethora of great resources that can help couples overcome obstacles in this area. This is not something to shy away from. On the contrary, the sexual component of your relationship deserves just as much time and attention as the emotional and spiritual.

We Must Protect Our Marriage with Healthy Boundaries

One of my biggest fears is being lost at sea, and after watching movies like Titanic, Cast Away, and The Perfect Storm, I believe I can make a water-tight case as to why it would be the worst thing ever. Being stranded miles from shore in shark-infested waters with no food or drinkable water, enduring the scorching sun or even a major storm while sustaining potentially life-threatening injuries . . . no thank you. And if all of that weren't bad enough, the worst part would be the aimless drifting, just bobbing along helpless and hopeless.

What does a boat lost at sea have to do with marriage? Without protection, each is vulnerable to the formidable elements that can quickly and easily overtake our vessel.

Just as the physical world has protective barriers and boundaries like doors, fences, road markers, and signs, our relational world needs the protection of safe boundaries, too. In their best-selling book series, Boundaries, authors Dr. Henry Cloud and Dr. John Townsend emphasize that "boundaries help us know where someone's control begins and ends." As with property lines, so it is with relationships. Your neighbor cannot come over and force you to paint your house, nor can your spouse "make" you do anything. But for love to exist and your marriage to be protected, you must maintain healthy, proper boundaries within your relationship.

Though not an exhaustive list, here are five necessary boundaries every marriage needs:

1. Work Boundaries. Understanding that men and women must work together in a professional environment warrants a conversation between partners. Our sons were lucky to have a mentor who emphasized an action called a "pre-choice choice," which means you have to decide ahead of time what you are going to do if you're presented with a compromising situation. That's why a conversation about co-workers, business travels, work expectations, and what you are both comfortable with while on the job is crucial in protecting your marriage.

2. Friendship Boundaries. We can hardly think of an exception where having friends of the opposite sex is healthy. Every affair starts out as "nothing" or "we're just friends." Whether you've been friends since first grade or not, it doesn't matter. You may think it's innocent, but your spouse may feel differently. Their feelings and opinions ought to hold more weight. Feelings of jealousy can arise quickly and cause unnecessary arguments and hurt. It's just not worth putting the integrity of your marriage at risk.

3. Personal Hobby Boundaries. When two become one, it doesn't mean we give up our rights as individuals. God gave each of us interests, talents, and passions we are to develop and pursue, whether it's hunting, creating, or exercising. We are meant to enjoy these with others, but if we don't set limits on how much time we spend away from our spouse, he/she can feel less of a priority, which weakens our boundary wall in the marriage.

4. Phone Boundaries. This is a big one. Even though we've mentioned it already, it bears repeating. When our kids were young we had a "Tech-No Day" of the week. It meant no technology for the evening. We had to "hang up and hang out" and we'd play games as a family or go visit friends or grandparents. They didn't like it at first but after a while, the kids actually looked forward to it! We have also learned the value of implementing "No Go Zones" for our iPhones that include the dinner table, bedroom, or if we are watching a movie together. We also try to clearly communicate when the other is in the middle of texting or doing something necessary on the phone by saying, "Let me know when you are finished so I can talk to you." That's the cue to finish up and put it down. And we can't forget to mention, sharing passwords is non-negotiable. Our spouse should feel comfortable checking email, social media accounts, text messages, etc. No secrets allowed.

5. Parenting Boundaries. Having the same expectations for the kids and sticking to them is one of the most important boundaries of all. Kids are really good at manipulating to get what they want and playing mom and dad against each other. Most likely, you and your spouse are not always going to agree in all situations but one thing you must stick to is the rule to disagree behind closed doors. Once the tiny humans sniff disunity, they will call mutiny! Backing each other up and sticking to your guns while disagreeing in private not only shows honor and respect, but it gives kids a strong foundation of security and is one of the best ways to implement a healthy boundary of protection for your marriage and family.

Chad is a former basketball coach who echoes what other good coaches have said: "the best offense is a good defense"— or is it the other way around?! Either way, both are equally important in playing the game. Protecting our spouse's reputation and sexual integrity and maintaining healthy boundaries is good defense and will help you win together in marriage.

22. Validation

Growing up, my dad was very witty, had a good sense of humor, and liked to tease a lot. I mean no disrespect, but sometimes his playful banter would cross the line and become hurtful, even critical. He would then try to brush it off by saying, "You only tease the ones you love." To this day, I bristle at that saying because it made me feel like he was disowning or minimizing the fact that he upset me. I felt dismissed, belittled, and invalidated.

Proverbs 12:18 says, "Some people make cutting remarks, but the words of the wise bring healing." Validation involves choosing your words thoughtfully and carefully while responding in supportive, positive ways that make your spouse feel cherished. Your words have the power to affirm your spouse's worth. Consequently, not only what you say, but how you say it has the capacity to pull your spouse close or push them away. Consider the following examples and decide if they are validating or invalidating responses:

<u>Spouse 1:</u>

"I'm upset because you were so late in picking up the kids."

<u>Spouse 2:</u>

"Get over it, it's not that big of a deal."

or

"I'm sorry, I lost track of time and was absorbed in my project at work."

<u>Spouse 1:</u>

"Our cat was hit by a car and I'm so sad."

<u>Spouse 2:</u>

"I'm sorry. I know how much you loved that thing. Maybe we can look to get another one?"

or

"Who cares? It's just a dumb cat."

Spouse 1:

"I'm bummed that I have to work over the holiday."

Spouse 2:

"I would be disappointed too."

or

"You should be glad it only happened this time, I never get a holiday off."

Spouse 1:

"I loved that movie! It was funny and entertaining. I really enjoyed it."

Spouse 2:

"It wasn't my favorite. In fact, I didn't like it at all, but I had fun watching you laugh."

or

"You have the dumbest sense of humor!"

Spouse 1:

"Did you hear what your mom said about my cooking? It really hurt my feelings."

Spouse 2:

"You are so emotional and take everything so personally . . . seriously."

or

"Who cares what she says? I love it and that's what matters!"

There are also derogatory, sarcastic comments and trite clichés such as:

- *You're overreacting; there's nothing to worry about.*

- *Why do you get so upset for no reason?*

- *Stop being a drama queen.*

- *You're always complaining; don't be so sensitive.*

- *I'm sorry I'm not perfect like you.*

- *Why can't you be more like . . . ?*

- *You just need to pray more.*

- *It could be worse; you should be more positive.*

These invalidating statements are extremely toxic intimacy killers. They don't serve to make our spouse feel cherished, and they definitely don't deepen intimacy—they destroy it!

Research shows that invalidation leads to isolation and is an accurate predictor of future problems—even divorce. Ultimately, the spouse receiving the invalidating comments is going to feel unheard, misunderstood, frustrated, angry, resentful, and bitter. If our goal is to deepen our intimacy, a good Scripture to keep in mind is Proverbs 15:1: "A gentle answer turns away wrath, but a harsh word stirs up anger."

A gentle, validating response is crucial, especially in highly charged moments, because it counteracts opposition with acceptance. It doesn't necessarily mean you agree with your partner's assumption, but you can still validate their feelings by responding empathetically and putting yourself in their shoes, making your spouse feel understood.

Here is a hypothetical example: If Chad is in a meeting and cannot answer his phone or text, I may think he is ignoring me, so I become frustrated and angry. When he finally calls me back, I justify why I am upset and explain I thought he was ignoring me on purpose. Factually, I am wrong, but my feelings have a valid point. A validating response would be, "Honey, I'd be upset, too, if I thought you were ignoring me, but I wasn't. I was talking to the boss and my phone was in my pocket." At this point, the frustration quickly drains away. A validating response means my spouse can disagree with my assumption while accepting (not belittling) my feelings in a significant way that makes me feel cherished.

Here are a few more validating responses:

- *I may not understand exactly what you are experiencing, but you have a right to your feelings.*
- *Help me fully understand how difficult this is for you so I know how to support you.*
- *I know this is hard for you to talk about. Take your time.*
- *I appreciate you letting me know because it hurts me to know I've upset you.*

Sometimes quiet listening is the best form of validation. Be present and ready to embrace with gentleness because what you don't say is sometimes just as important as what you do say . . . which leads to the next point.

Validating with Our Actions

If you've ever been on the receiving end of another driver's nonverbal expression of anger (ahem, flipping of the bird), you know the effectiveness of body language. That action alone is proof that nonverbal communication speaks a language of its own that, in many ways, can be richer and more effective than our words. It is estimated that sixty to ninety percent of communication is expressed through our body, so it is important to understand that validating our spouse requires using more than correct or validating words. Our gestures, facial expressions, and posture all play a huge role in cherishing our spouse.

If there is one gesture that sends Chad over the edge more than any other, it is the ol' eye roll. And while I have been known to insert it during arguments, it is the equivalent to throwing gasoline on a kindled fire. Stand back, because he is about to explode! Honestly, I don't blame him because there are few gestures more disrespectful than an eye roll. Some other negative postures we must give nod to are folded arms, fidgeting, turning your body away from your spouse when they are talking, sassy, sarcastic facial expressions, and slumped posture. We already touched on the importance of eye contact, so as previously stated, staring at your phone while your spouse is talking also communicates they are not a priority.

On the flip side, there are positive, validating body movements that convey that you cherish your spouse, but you need to be intentional about expressing them. For example, an open stance with your arms relaxed and not crossed or folded, regular eye contact, engaging facial expressions, and upright posture (no slouched shoulders) communicate, "You matter to me and I am interested in what you are saying." By doing so, your spouse feels validated and cherished.

Validation is a Skill

What we have just covered may seem like common sense. While it may appear simple in theory, validation is a skill that can turn into an art with a little practice. If you are more introverted or if healthy communication habits were not modeled in your home when you were growing up, validating your spouse may not come naturally. For others, such as someone who is a "people person," it may come a little easier.

Either way, we can always get better. Because validation requires effort it can seem forced, fake, or even condescending to say "rehearsed phrases," like "I'm sorry you feel that way" when you are used to saying, "Stop being dramatic." But the more we do it, the more authentic and genuine it becomes.

When we learn to combine validating phrases with positive body language, our Emotional IQ skyrockets and our intimacy deepens because we are creating a safe environment of acceptance in our relationship. We are communicating to our spouse that they matter. They are valued. Treasured. Loved. Cherished.

To Love and To Cherish

Our wedding vow "to love and to cherish" is such an exhaustive topic that it is impossible to cover all the ground. You've probably noticed that we've spent most of our time on the emotional and physical aspects, which most people think of when they hear the word intimacy. But as we've already established, to experience intimacy on the deepest level, we need to connect in all three areas—the emotional, physical, and spiritual. Even if a couple has a good emotional and physical connection, the spiritual aspect of intimacy is often the missing

link to a successful marriage, which is where our next action

step leads us.

23. Pursue God Together

Jeff and Cheryl Scruggs are the founders of Hope Matters Marriage Ministries in Dallas, Texas. Both Jeff and Cheryl are marriage counselors who share their story in a real and raw way in their book, I Do Again: How We Found Our Second Chance at Marriage—and You Can Too. Their marriage journey is one of restoration, reconciliation, and redemption as they were married, divorced, then later remarried to each other. In the book they share the difference between their first and second marriage - Jesus at the center. Their story is an engaging read where you cannot help but see God's hand at work and realize how nurturing all three aspects of our being are necessary for a fulfilling marriage.

Jeff and Cheryl's story emphasizes that God's heart beats with a desire to be included in marriage. Just like He was with Adam and Eve, He wants to be at the center of your relationship, too. Sure, you can have a good marriage through commitment and effort alone. But we aren't after just "good." We are pursuing the best possible marriage we can have. We yearn for a deeply intimate and mutually satisfying connection that is beyond the natural realm! We are after God's best, which requires inviting Him to transform us through His loving presence and His unlimited power.

Using your imagination, picture that three-legged stool again. God is the third leg in your relationship. Without Him, your marriage will be wobbly and unstable at best. He is the one who ultimately holds us together, brings stability, and provides protection from outside attacks that threaten to tear us apart.

King Solomon says it best in Ecclesiastes 4:12, "A person standing alone can be attacked and defeated, but two can stand back to back and conquer. Three are even better for a triple-braided cord is not easily broken."

God's influence is the missing link. If you absolutely want to take intimacy with your spouse to a deeper, more fulfilling level, focus on the spiritual aspect first by pursuing a personal relationship with God. When you cherish Him above all else, even your spouse, and you align your heart with His heart and order your life around His way of doing things, you'll become the person your spouse is naturally drawn to. Your relationship with God through the Holy Spirit will soften those rough edges and turn you into the man or woman He created you to be and the partner your husband or wife needs. Like the three points on a triangle, the closer both of you draw to God at the top, the closer you will draw to each other.

We have emphasized praying together, but pursuing God also involves reading His Word together. Consider Hebrews 4:12 – "For the word of God is full of living power. It is sharper than the sharpest knife, cutting deep into our innermost thoughts and desires. It exposes us for what we really are" (emphasis added).

Have you ever had the following thoughts? "I feel disconnected from my spouse." "I don't know what to do about this issue that we can't seem to get past." "I am unsure if what I want to do is the right thing." "We need help in this situation." Glance back at the verse above. What is the Word of God full of? Living power! Scripture contains the power to change not only our external situations but guide our internal thoughts by exposing the truth of what is going on in and around us.

God speaks directly through His Word and when each spouse is reading the same passage, it's like double the power! I may uncover a truth that Chad didn't see, and he may receive an insight that I hadn't known, and when we put those together, we gain clarity. Our hearts become tied together in unity of thought and purpose. We gain traction as we recalibrate our direction toward the future God has mapped out for us. The fact that God speaks to us with heavenly wisdom that transcends our human limitations is truly mind blowing.

The best part is that God doesn't reserve His blessings for a select few with a squeaky-clean past or present saintly behavior. The transformative power that flows through His Word is available to every one of us. Our marriage and yours. The only prerequisite is that we intentionally seek Him. In His own words found in the book of Jeremiah, God proclaims, "I am the LORD, the God of all the peoples of the world. Is anything too hard for me? . . . Ask me and I will tell you some remarkable secrets . . ." (Jeremiah 32:27 and Jeremiah 33:3 NLT). What an encouragement for us to dig into His Word!

Chad and I have found the YouVersion app on our phones to be a helpful tool in pursuing God through His Word. The app provides a plethora of Bible reading plans covering a wide range of topics from marriage, forgiveness, anxiety, and much, much more. We read through different plans during our morning coffee time. The app allows you to comment on what you just read, which is a non-threatening way to be vulnerable and known spiritually. The app also provides a point of reference to have a follow-up discussion later so we can hold each other accountable. We also love the fact that we do not have to necessarily be together to read together. That is probably the most common obstacle a lot of couples face— carving out time to read the Bible together. In our opinion, YouVersion is the perfect place to start if you've never read Scripture together before.

Do what works for you, but to go deep, you must be intentional. Cherishing our spouse deepens intimacy. It involves managing the tension by nurturing all three aspects of the person—the emotional, physical, and spiritual. When you pursue God you are positioning yourself to reap an exciting, deeply fulfilling, intimate relationship with your spouse that cannot be found anywhere else in the world!

Questions to Consider:

1. Your spouse loves you, but do you feel your spouse cherishes you? Why or why not?

2. List three things you can do to demonstrate how much you cherish your spouse.

3. Have you set healthy boundaries in your marriage? If not, where can you start?

236

Notes:

V.

Until Death Do Us Part

Maintaining Commitment

Continual adjustments are necessary to ensure my marriage lasts.

24. Happily "Never" After

Below is a compiled list of *Ten Things You Never Hear People Say*. See you if agree with these statements:

10. Isn't it great the airline lost our luggage?!

9. What's Facebook?

8. Get off the phone, I need to use the internet.

7. That business meeting was so fun and full of useful, relevant information; I wish it would have lasted another hour!

6. Let me go look up their number in the phone book.

5. I love getting stuck in traffic.

4. I cannot wait to spend every holiday with my in-laws!

3. Did you pack the camcorder?

2. Honey, when I am upset and you tell me to just relaaaaax, it really calms me down.

1. (Couples standing at the altar on their wedding day) I do hope we get divorced someday.

Some of the statements are simply out of date, while others are just irrational. I cannot think of the last time I lugged around a camcorder like a television news reporter or looked up a friend's phone number in an actual phone book. And who says they love getting stuck in traffic or sitting in a business meeting that has gone past its allotted time frame? No one. Ever.

Arguably, the most ridiculous of them all would be number one. Have you ever been to a wedding where, after the couple says, "I do" they complete the sentence with "hope this lasts only a few years"? Or "I do intend for this relationship to eventually fall apart"? Honestly, we have been to our fair share of weddings over the years and no one has said, "I hope we live happily never after!" On the contrary, there are smiles and tears of joy as couples stand face-to-face, beaming with hope-filled excitement. They believe their dreams and desires for an intimate, fulfilling relationship are not only on the precipice of coming true, but will last a lifetime too.

For this very reason, in our vows we promise to love each other "until death do us part." We want to go the distance with this person and build a life and legacy that is enduring and endearing. The good news is that God is on our side as He wants the same thing. His heart is spelled out so clearly several places in Scripture:

> *"A wife is married to her husband as long as he lives. If her husband dies, she is free to marry whomever she wishes . . . ." (1 Corinthians 7:39 NLT)*

> *"When a woman marries, the law binds her to her husband as long as he is alive. But if he dies, the laws of marriage no longer apply to her." (Romans 7:2 NLT)*

God's Word is clear. His design and plan from the beginning was one man plus one woman for one lifetime. Please know that if you are divorced and remarried there is no shame, guilt, or condemnation written in these pages, so please do not go there. Our hope and encouragement are that you take what is here and move forward. You may be one who, through past, personal experience, understands the importance of this message more than anyone and can inspire someone else who is struggling. What a wonderful reality that no matter where we have been, we can move forward in the grace God so freely gives.

For some, God's ideal might sound ridiculous or even impossible, but neither are the case. When we do things God's way, good things happen. All of His ways are simple, meaning they are straightforward and plain enough we can understand them without a scholarly explanation, but they are not necessarily easy in the sense that results are not achieved without effort. His principles are not always convenient, comfortable, or fun, but we have to keep in mind: What comes easy does not last, and what lasts does not come easy. A lifelong marriage takes some serious effort and commitment, but like a fine wine, marriage gets better with time!

Think of a lasting marriage as similar to the lifespan of a vehicle. At the time of purchase, as you drive your brand-new car off the lot, you hold to the ideal that it is going to stay new forever. You vow to preserve its mint condition by keeping that new car smell and those shiny rims, and you certainly will not allow kids to leave smashed fries in the creases or fingerprints on the windows! Your enthusiastic goals are to make sure the engine runs at optimal levels and to keep the exterior free of scratches and dents! But are those things going to happen without any effort on your part?

To maximize the life of your vehicle, you're going to have to practice routine maintenance. You will definitely need to vacuum the inside—suck up the fries and the dirt from baseball cleats, wipe the dust off the dash, and run it through the car wash regularly. Don't forget to schedule oil changes, fill your washer fluid, and change the air filter. And be careful where you park so other cars do not ding your doors.

We know we have to take responsibility to maintain the life of our car, but are all of these things necessarily easy? No, they require effort. It is not always convenient to take time out of your schedule to get an oil change. No one enjoys grabbing a dirty hose at the gas station and vacuuming in 40-degree weather, and you'll probably have to walk a little further if you park away from other cars, which takes additional time and energy. All of these actions are simple adjustments but will require effort if we want to maintain the longevity of our vehicle.

Those who have been married more than five minutes can attest that the reality of marriage is not always sparkly and shiny. We are selfish people who sling muddy, hurtful words at times. Each of us has unique ways of denting our spouse's fenders and dinging their doors. Like a stray baseball that shatters our car window, we don't (usually) intentionally inflict damage. But as much as we want our marriage to be ideal, reality gets in the way!

I loved playing house as a little girl, dreaming about what my life would look like one day. But when I grew up I realized that I did not include some real-life issues in my pretend play.

I did not have dirty dishes in my play kitchen sink and there were no bills piled on the counter in my dollhouse. I could make the babies stop crying whenever I wanted, and my plastic, pretend husband did whatever I told him to. I didn't incorporate any difficult, unexpected, life-altering circumstances that threatened to make me want to quit my pretend play, either.

Truth be told, my grown-up reality does not always match my eight-year-old ideal. For some, that alone is enough to discourage commitment. But if that is not reason enough to quit, our culture sure does not offer any help either. The primary message that comes from movies, magazines, and media says that our motivation to maintain commitment in marriage depends on our level of happiness which, in turn, is based on our spouse's performance. There is very little in our culture today that encourages couples to make the required adjustments that are necessary for our marriage to last "until death do us part."

Consider this question before we move on: How much effort are you willing to exert to ensure the longevity of your marriage? We touched on vehicle maintenance, but what about marriage maintenance? What can we do on a regular basis to make sure our marriage lasts a lifetime? The principles of car maintenance also apply to marriage maintenance: continual adjustments create the desired result. The desired result we are after is to fulfill our vows, enjoy a mutually satisfying relationship, and make our marriage last "until death do us part!" You do not drive your car off the lot and get one oil change, vacuum it once a year, or put gas in when you feel like it. You do these things frequently. So, let's look at some necessary adjustments we need to make on a regular basis.

25. Adjust Our Attitude

Both of us were born and raised in Michigan, so Chad and I are die-hard Detroit Lions fans—which means you are either one of us, laugh at us, or feel sorry for us. We are blissfully hopeful that someday they might make it to a Super Bowl but in the meantime, we've had to live vicariously through other winning teams like the New England Patriots when Tom Brady was their quarterback. Our affinity is due partly to Tom Brady's University of Michigan ties, but also because he instinctively knows how to win. I know, I know, there are probably some haters but regardless of your personal feelings (and setting aside Deflategate), how about we let Tom Brady's stats speak for themselves? The list is quite impressive.

- Seven-time Super Bowl Champion

- Five-time Super Bowl MVP

- He is a three-time NFL Most Valuable Player

- Named the NFL Comeback Player of the Year

- Associated Press Male Athlete of the Year

- Sports Illustrated Sportsman of the Year

After watching a documentary on Tom's road to success, I was impressed by his enthusiasm, drive, and commitment for the game. But what really caught my attention was a statement he made that gave away his winning secret. It was not anything deeply profound; he just said, "I'm going to do whatever it takes, no matter what, to win." As I watched the rest of his story, I saw this attitude reflected in his daily routine and intentional actions.

Despite the fact that his athleticism looks so natural and he has been in the NFL for twenty plus years, Tom Brady continues to watch film for hours on end and has a personal training coach who continually instructs him regarding his technique. He welcomes constructive criticism and then implements the coach's suggestions during hours of repetition on the practice field. Many times, he is the last one to leave practice. He also takes care of his body with precise detail, which is evident in his healthy eating habits and regular sleep schedule. Most of us look at that and say, "Wow, that's a picture of true commitment!" And I believe it is. Do you have the same level of commitment when it comes to your marriage?

True Vs. False Commitment

When someone says, "I'm committed to my marriage," how do we know it's true? Many people have said that, but reality shows otherwise (again, I realize there are many different factors and scenarios in all sorts of situations from abuse to affairs, so we are moving forward in grace and speaking about commitment in a general sense). I'm suggesting that there is a difference between True and False Commitment:

True Commitment has the "I will do whatever it takes to make this marriage last" attitude.

False Commitment says "I really like this and want it to continue."

True Commitment is based on a fixed attitude.

False Commitment is based on fluctuating feelings.

I read a news article a few years ago that revealed a rising cultural trend that couples are choosing to write their own wedding vows. Some promise to also love and cherish their partner's dog or cat, while others are choosing to reconstruct the traditional vows like the ones we have been discussing. Instead of "until death do us part," some have reworded it to say, "as long as our love shall last," or "until our time together is over." Here is the evidence proving their false commitment, which is based on fluctuating feelings.

What these couples are really exposing is that their commitment is not only false, but it is also extremely selfish. These misleading phrases are the exact opposite of a rock-solid promise to express true, unconditional, sacrificial love toward another person. Rather, their "love" is focusing inward. They're looking out for their own interests, needs, and feelings, which is the exact opposite of God's definition. The truth is you cannot have a lifelong love with your spouse if you are in love with yourself! Sadly, it is a struggle we all face because of our human nature. Where self-love is focused inward, true, sacrificial love is focused outward toward our spouse. True commitment is selfless. There is a huge difference between, "I'll ride this thing as long as I'm happy and you are meeting my expectations," and "until death do us part." True commitment really is quite clear that the only thing that will come between or separate us is, well, death itself.

Allow me to gently ask again: What is your attitude toward commitment in marriage? This is a question that requires honest, purposeful reflection. If we want a love that lasts, we need to adjust our attitude and make sure we are of the "do whatever it takes" attitude instead of "do whatever I feel."

How Do We Develop the Attitude of True Commitment?

The fixed attitude of true commitment that says "I'm going to do whatever it takes to make my marriage last a lifetime" is not going to come easy or naturally—but God showed us it is possible if we follow Jesus's example that Paul shares in Philippians 2:5:

"Your attitude should be the same that Christ Jesus had. Though He was God, he did not demand and cling to his rights as God. He made himself nothing; he took the humble position of a slave and appeared in human form. And in human form he obediently humbled himself even further by dying a criminal's death on a cross. . . ."

Jesus's "whatever it takes" attitude was completely selfless. He gave up His home and rights in heaven and went all the way to the cross to make sure we could have a relationship with God here and now and forever into eternity. That is how much God loves us! But it did not come easily; it required humility on Jesus's part. The Son of God understood what was necessary to bring about this desired result—a restored relationship with humanity. As Hebrews 12 says,

"He was willing to die a shameful death on the cross because of the joy he knew would be his afterward. He made a way for us to come back to God and now he's seated next to him in the place of highest honor."

Seated on His throne in heaven's perfection, Jesus could have said to God the Father, "That's not in my best interest. That is going to hurt too much, cost too much" instead He humbly and selflessly chose the "I'll do whatever it takes" attitude of humility by putting our needs ahead of His own. Pastor Rick Warren sums up the essence of humility and says is not "thinking less of yourself, but thinking of yourself less." That is precisely what Jesus did.

What Does Humility in Marriage Look Like?

Remember elementary school when the cool thing was to get chosen to be the "line leader" for the day? You felt important and in charge . . . but grown-up humility is a race to the back of the line. It insists "you go first" while at the same time asks, "How can I help?"

Imagine your spouse asking that question during your morning coffee time together or walking through the door after work, tossing the car keys on the counter and inquiring, "What can I do for you?" How would you feel? Now flip the scenario around. How would your spouse react if you did the same?

What do you think the landscape of your marriage would look like if each of you were continually doing "whatever it took" to make sure the other person was cared for and their needs were met first? How would the atmosphere in your home improve? Less tension? More joy? Less stress? More laughter? Can you picture the transforming effect it would have on your relationship if each of you were putting the other person's needs ahead of your own, displaying humility on a daily basis?

Adjusting our attitude to "I'm going to do whatever it takes to make this relationship last" requires humility—being spouse-focused rather than self-focused—and helps us maintain true commitment.

26. Adjust Our Allowances

You have probably heard the phrase, "There's no 'I' in team, but there is 'me.'" It is a tongue-in-cheek saying that conveys the message that one individual is more important than the combined effort of the group. If you have ever played a team sport of any kind, you know just how detrimental, not to mention annoying, this kind of attitude can be, as it completely dismantles team unity. The goal becomes less about fulfilling a shared vision and more about individual glory.

I am not competitive. I am sensitive by nature, so I always feel bad for the player who costs the team the game-winning point. One summer day, while we were still in college, I vividly remember visiting Chad's family for the weekend when his family decided to play a backyard game of volleyball. I never played volleyball on an official, organized team but assumed I could hang with Chad, his dad, and two brothers as it would be just a fun little game of tossing the ball back and forth.

Wrong.

A serve came at me like a speeding bullet, and I ducked as the ball bounced at my feet. I was stunned and then shocked as his dad yelled and pointed at me, "When he moves over, you move up!" I wanted to walk off and cry. I will never forget the shock and embarrassment I felt. Perhaps from this experience, I now empathize with a player who "falls short." Whether it comes down to a field goal or a free throw to clinch the game, I feel sorry for the teammate who misses the shot. As if that is not humiliating enough, to make matters worse, the sports shows on TV play the mistake over and over as a highlight. Even though technically it is a team effort, sometimes it comes down to one player literally "dropping the ball."

The same holds true in marriage. Each spouse is an equal member on a two-person team that shares the same goal—to achieve a lasting and fulfilling marriage as the desired result. And even though we are working together toward our shared vision, there will be times when our teammate lets us down and we let them down. Our team is made up of two imperfect people who have bad days, who sometimes slack off, and are weaker in different areas. But at the end of the day, it doesn't change the fact that we are still a team.

What Are We to Do?

According to Colossians 3:13, when our teammate lets us down, the best thing to do is to adjust our allowances:

"You must make allowances for each other's faults and forgive the person who offends you. Remember, the Lord forgave you, so you must forgive others."

It is not a shocking discovery to hear our spouse has faults, is it? What's appalling is to admit we have them, too! It is interesting that "faults" in the original Greek language means "an occasion to complain." Does your spouse ever give you an occasion to complain? Do you give your spouse an occasion to complain?

If I asked you to get out a piece of paper and write down five things your spouse does that irritate you, you quite possibly could rattle off a list without giving it much thought. But if I asked you to write down your top five faults, perhaps you would have a harder time. I am not necessarily talking about the big things like personality or character issues; I am referring to the silly little everyday pet peeves or bad habits that can really bug us and get under our skin, like leaving underwear on the bathroom floor after a shower or my habit of cracking eggs and leaving the broken shells in the carton so, at a glance, it looks like we have a dozen eggs when we really have only two left. Maybe you're a husband with a wife who leaves her bobby pins all over the bathroom counter. Perhaps you're a wife who gets frustrated when your husband never leaves his keys in the same place.

Bottom line: We all have faults. No one is exempt from giving their spouse an "occasion to complain." Every one of us, even the easy-going, even-tempered, good-natured people have a breaking point where they get irritated over little things. No matter what they are, though, Paul says we are to "make allowances" for them. In the original Greek language, it means we are to forbear: "show restraint, to hold oneself back, don't proceed, resist temptation to respond." That is to be our response, to adjust our behavior toward the little things our spouse does that irritate us. A good rule of thumb when it comes to faults is to "pass over rather than point out." Pointing out leads to provocation. Passing over leads to peace.

Abigail, A Beauitful Example

There is a wonderful example in Scripture of a lovely woman who had "many occasions to complain," and then some. Her name is Abigail, and she was married to an evil, wicked man named Nabal. Her story is found in 1 Samuel 25 and describes Nabal as a wealthy man who is mean and dishonest in all his dealings (honestly, the guy was a real jerk and crook). Abigail was sensible and beautiful. Their story intersects with David (before he was King David) who had a message delivered to Nabal asking him to return a favor. Earlier, when David and his men were in the wilderness they camped next to Nabal's property and protected his flocks from harm. Now David and his men were in need and felt it was only fair for Nabal to pay back their good deed.

Instead, Nabal, being a wicked and evil jerk, went ballistic. He basically said, "I don't know who you are or care and I'm not giving you anything, so get out of here!" You can imagine how enraged David was, and rightly so. Preparing for retaliation, David told four hundred of his men to strap on their swords. His exact words were, "May God deal with me severely if even one man of his household is still alive tomorrow morning!"

Word got to Abigail, who was alarmed, and she quickly planned to intercede. She hastily gathered a bunch of food and went out to meet the entourage. When she met up with David, she fell at his feet and gave an Oscar award-winning speech of a lifetime! Basically, she begged for her life and home to be spared . . . and it worked! David's anger diffused and he told her to return to her home in peace and they would not seek revenge. Hold on . . . the story gets even better!

When Abigail arrived home, she found Nabal drunk from partying, oblivious to anything that had just happened. Talk about making allowances for this guy's faults, which were more than just pet peeves—this woman put up with a LOT. She could have confronted him and said, "You jerk! Don't you know that what you just did was a slap in the face? I saved your sorry self and our entire household while you sat and drank yourself into a stupor!" Instead, she showed a tremendous amount of restraint.

At the risk of sounding like the voice on an infomercial, "But wait! There's more!" The ending to the story is epic! The next morning, when Nabal was finally sober, Abigail told him what happened. As a result, he had a stroke and was paralyzed until he died ten days later! When David heard Nabal was dead, he declared, "Praise the Lord who has paid back Nabal and kept me from doing it myself." Then he wasted no time in sending messengers to Abigail to ask her to become his wife!

What a "happily ever after" ending that resulted from Abigail's actions, which proves that "passing over rather than pointing out leads to peace." As we conclude Abigail's telling tale, glance back to Colossians 3:13 and notice how Paul takes it yet one step further in the second part of the verse, where he says, "and forgive the person who offends you."

The Adjustment of Forgiveness

While there are trivial, little things that irritate and frustrate us in our marriage, there will also be "big things" that are going to require us to extend forgiveness, and times when we will be the ones who need to ask for forgiveness. A lasting, "until death do us part" marriage is made up of two good forgivers. No healthy marriage can last without it.

No doubt about it, forgiveness is hard. But there are many false assumptions, poor excuses, and warped misconceptions around the action that keep us trapped in bitterness and misery. Some people think that if you forgive, you also have to forget or it's letting the other person off the hook too easily. As humans, we categorize what offenses "deserve" forgiveness because we deem some violations as simply unforgivable. Others rationalize and justify that, "I'm not God. I don't have the power or ability to forgive" because the pain is so great. Forgiveness is hard.

All that aside, Jesus made a big deal about forgiving. He never categorized or excused offenses. He simply told us that no matter the offense, it is in our best interest to forgive the person who hurt us. Each situation is different. Sometimes forgiveness happens instantaneously. Other times, it is a process. In either case, the essence of forgiveness is choosing not to hold or use the offense against the other person. I am not going to carry around a scorecard to keep a tally of wrongs my spouse does and save them up to use as ammunition later.

When you forgive, you are simply trusting that the Lord, in His time and in His way, will make things right. It does not always mean instant reconciliation, especially if a big breach of confidence has been broken. Forgiveness does not automatically reinstate trust into the relationship. Trust takes time to be rebuilt. Boundaries must be established. But the evil, unseen enemy of your marriage would like you to believe that your spouse shouldn't be forgiven, doesn't deserve to be forgiven, while at the same time convincing you that holding onto your anger and bitterness will keep you safe from further betrayal or pain. Please, let me gently encourage you by saying if that is the case, those thoughts are not bringing healing to your marriage but are causing the wound to fester.

Discussing forgiveness requires more time and space than these pages allow, but the point we can all grasp is that you don't have to be married for very long to know that each of you will be on the giving or receiving end of forgiveness. "Making allowances for one another's faults and forgiving the person who offends us" are necessary adjustments we must make if we want our marriage to last.

27. Adjust Our Allies

Tom Brady did not win seven Super Bowls by himself. He had coaches, receivers, linemen, and kickers who all supported him in his efforts as quarterback. It takes an enormous amount of people to accomplish a Super Bowl victory. There is no way Tom Brady could do it alone, and we cannot win in marriage without a good team around us.

Consider your social circle. Who do you choose to surround yourself with? Who are your friends, the people you invest your time and energy in? Our friends are different from our family in the sense that friends are in our lives because we chose to give them a seat at our table. We invited them in because they enriched our lives for the better. The goal is to have friends that make your marriage better and make you better at marriage!

Friends have such an influential role in our lives that the Bible warns us about who we should choose. 1 Corinthians 15:33 says that "bad company corrupts good character." Those we allow to influence us is something we need to be very mindful of. We watched a heartbreaking scenario play out in a marriage that was extremely close to us. The wife started going out after work once in a while with a certain group of co-workers, then it turned into hanging out with them on weekends. They started drinking more and she began spending more time away from her husband and kids. Just as the Bible warns that we run the risk of becoming like the people we hang out with, that is precisely what happened. The wife started changing her habits and these friends eventually influenced her to leave her husband, and they got divorced.

It is extremely important to choose wisely who we surround ourselves with and keep as our allies. Bad company does corrupt good character, but it's also true that good company can guard us from the bad. Perhaps you are familiar with the following exercise often taught to students: One student is asked to stand on a chair while another stands next to him on the ground. As they grab hold of each other's hand, the question is asked, "Is it easier for the person standing on the chair to pull the other up or the one standing on the ground to pull the other down?" The answer is, "It is easier to pull the one off the chair down." This shows the importance of having like minded friends, those who adhere to similar values and will cheer your marriage on.

Healthy Friendships are a Blessing

Healthy friendships are a gift from God and come with a whole lot of benefits. Medical studies show that couples with healthy friendships outside of marriage and those who are active in a community—especially a faith community—have better overall physical health. They experience strengthened immune systems, decreased stress levels, and sharper brains due to varying conversations and interactions. Combining these benefits together, they serve to increase our life expectancy, which naturally means a longer marriage!

Some of our best memories include our friends, Todd and Sheila, who we randomly met at a restaurant while celebrating my Grandma's 80th birthday when our now grown son was a baby in a car seat. Chad and Todd struck up a conversation across the tables (probably about a basketball game that was on the TV), and shortly after our paths crossed again when we ended up attending the same church. That was the starting point of our friendship that has lasted more than twenty years. We have enjoyed camping together, traveling on family vacations together, and spending time at each other's houses just hanging out. Through the years, we have celebrated the birth of more children and now we are on to sharing weddings and grandchildren. The best part is that even though we now live far apart, we can pick up right where we left off and not skip a beat! We treasure Todd and Sheila and consider them lifelong friends, as we have walked side-by-side through some pretty tough times together. They have enriched our lives and our marriage in countless ways through their lasting support. Good friends, like them and other "couple friends" in our lives, are like four-leaf clovers—hard to find but lucky to have!

Not only are couple friends invaluable, but same sex friendships are important too as women need other women and guys need other guys. Proverbs 27:27 says, "As iron sharpens iron, a friend sharpens a friend."

My girlfriends support me in ways my husband cannot. Let's be honest, Chad is never going to understand what it's like to go through childbirth or experience hot flashes, nor does he know what it's like to be a mother-in-law. He can try to understand and empathize, but an "I get it" from a girlfriend can breathe fresh life into my spirit and bring comfort in ways he is incapable of, simply because he is a man. Vice versa, I cannot relate to what it's like to feel the adrenaline rush of watching geese circle a field and come close enough to shoot (and if I'm honest, I don't really want to, either). I can try, but Chad's hunting buddies relish those times, and they celebrate after spending a day in a field together. Girlfriends and guy friends enhance our lives by supporting us in different ways than our spouse because we share the same gender experiences.

Friends also keep us grounded in reality. They have the vantage point of being on the outside looking in, and are often able to provide a perspective we might not see. It is far easier for them to see our blind spots and, depending on the depth of friendship, they are better positioned to say things to us that we might receive differently if coming from our spouse. Their unique perspective, coupled with having our best interest at heart, keeps us living in the real world and not some pretend, fantasy land we either made up in our head or found online.

I was part of a group of ladies that got together pretty regularly and one of our friends began talking about a guy she met online who lived in another country. At first we were not too concerned, but then as more time went on and she talked about their interactions, the rest of us looked around with darting eyes and furrowed brows. She made comments about how her husband didn't like her innocent, budding overseas friendship, but every time he said something she blew him off or would get mad. We finally said that we agreed with him and did not think this was good—like, at all! We helped her see the situation for what it really was; unhealthy and potentially dangerous.

Healthy friendships help us to become better by giving grace when we stumble and truth when we stray. Do you have friends who have your best interest at heart? Do you allow them to speak truth to you? If you really want to dig deep and go for growth, ask your friend to tell you something you do not want to hear but need to hear. An interesting discussion is sure to follow; just make sure you are prepared to hear what they have to say!

As spouses, we need to encourage each other to develop healthy friendships. God made us to need friends—some more than others, so it is important to talk with our spouses about how much of a need each other has. Usually one person in the relationship is an extrovert and the other is an introvert, so one might require more "friend time" to feel rejuvenated. A sign of a healthy friendship is that you feel energized and encouraged after spending time with the other person. Talk to each other about your friends and decide what is best for you and your marriage.

Find a Mentor Couple

Another type of friendship that is unique and extremely beneficial in helping us maintain our commitment is to find a mentor couple—a husband and wife team who are older than you and just a lap or two ahead of you on your marriage journey. If you are in the baby stage, find a couple with elementary-aged kids. If you have teenagers raiding your fridge and coming in during the midnight hour, seek out empty nesters. Mentors are God's way of supporting and strengthening our marriage in a way that is exclusively different from our friends or parents. It is very hard to get an unbiased opinion from a family member like your mom, dad, sister, or even a friend who knows your entire history.

Being a parent of married children, I know I have to be careful to be fair and open-minded, and not automatically jump to the defense of my child, because no matter how old my son or daughter is, blood runs thick. I am not saying it is impossible to get solid advice from loved ones or that we shouldn't seek counsel from our friends and parents, but one benefit a mentor couple provides is that they come without any preconceived notions or attachments that might cloud their judgements.

As a neutral party, a mentor couple can provide a safe place to explore all the facets of marriage, since they are concerned for both of you equally and desire the success of your marriage. When paired with the right couple, the connection is a beautiful bond of sharing struggles and successes by learning from someone else's mistakes and milestones. Experience is the best teacher and the wisdom and insight that a mentor couple offers is priceless.

If seeking out or becoming a mentor couple sounds slightly intimidating, don't sweat. It does not have to be anything formal. No need to sign a contract. Truth be told, it is best to let it grow organically. If you are involved in a church or community where you've watched a certain couple interact with each other, or maybe you've heard a little of their story and think you might like to get to know them on a deeper level, invite them to go out for coffee or have them over for dessert. Again, nothing fancy. No reason to let this concept scare you, because you do not have to be perfect. No one is expecting anyone to have all the answers; just be open to the idea and test the waters.

Finally, mentoring is a lifestyle encouraged in Scripture. Paul was a mentor to many, including a man named Titus, whom he calls his true child in the faith. He wrote in his letter to Titus:

> "Teach the older women to live in a way that is appropriate for someone serving the Lord . . . _these older women must train the younger women_ to love their husbands and their children, to live wisely and be pure, to take care of their homes, to do good and to be submissive to their husbands . . . In the same way, _encourage the young men_ to live wisely in all they do and you yourself must _be an example_ to them by doing good deeds of every kind . . . ." (Titus 2:3a,4-5a,6,7a NLT, emphasis added)

No matter where we are on our journey, we are older than some couples and younger than others. That means we can be a mentor and have a mentor during every season of life.

Take some time to reflect on your friendships. Pray about them. Ask God to bring an "older than you couple" your way that can mentor you and a "younger than you" couple that you can influence and encourage. If we want to maintain our commitment "until death do us part," we will need a team of allies to help and support us every step of the way.

28. Press On Together

When it comes to maintaining our commitment, no couple is able to make it on their own. We were not designed to live without community. We need friends and mentors to guide us, instruct us, support us, encourage us, cheer for us when we succeed, and prod us back on track when we veer off course. The institution of marriage is under an all-out assault in our culture, so it is imperative we draw strength from others to keep going and keep fighting until we achieve our desired result, a fulfilling and enjoyable marriage that lasts "until death do us part."

Marriage is a journey. At the starting point we promise, "I do," and the goal is to cross the finish line and hear, "Well done." By God's grace and with support from each other, we will finish the race, hear those encouraging words, and experience eternal rewards.

None of us has it all figured out! Finishing well will not come without effort. Great marriages do not just happen. They take work, and sometimes blood, sweat, and many tears. Most importantly, we must be intentional. The Apostle Paul shares a moment of transparency in Philippians 3:13-14 when he reveals, "straining toward what is ahead, I press on toward the goal to win the prize for which God has called me heavenward in Christ Jesus." He doesn't mince any words or mislead us into believing that this life or our marriage is a walk in the park.

But he does encourage us to PRESS ON . . . keep doing the right things by choosing to adjust our attitude, saying, "I'm going to do whatever it takes to make my marriage last."

As we rely on God's grace with our eyes on the prize, we adjust our allowances for our spouse's faults by reminding ourselves to pass over, not point out, every little thing. In the big things, with God's help we choose the way of forgiveness, and as we vow to adjust our allies, we surround ourselves with healthy, life-giving friends and mentors who will encourage us to maintain our commitment.

What Will Your Marriage Look Like if You Make these Adjustments?

May we encourage you to PRESS ON. Keep going no matter where you are in your marriage journey. We can do so with confidence "that we will reap a harvest of blessing at the appropriate time if we don't give up!" (Galatians 6:9) Continual adjustments will bring about the desired result and with the help of God and those around you, your marriage can last "until death do us part."

Questions to Consider:

1. Do you use the "D" word (divorce) during arguments? Why or why not?

2. What area—Attitude, Allowances or Allies—needs to be adjusted in your marriage?

3. Have you ever been mentored by someone? Would you consider being a mentor to another couple? Why or why not?

Notes:

Conclusion

Writing a book is certainly a difficult process. Writing a book about your own journey that includes reflecting upon your mistakes and failures is definitely grueling. But recalling the lessons learned and seeing the progress in how far we've come has been totally rewarding. It's kind of like seeing "before and after" pictures of a person's weight loss journey! I love to witness the transformation which is evidence of how their hard work has paid off. In a similar way, hopefully you've been able to use your imagination to paint a vivid picture of our marriage "before and after". That's not to say we are the cover model for picture perfect relational health. We still have more room to grow in many ways. But as we rest at mile marker 30 on our journey, we've been able to reflect back and discover what - or more importantly - Who has brought us this far. God has poured His unconditional love and undeserved grace so lavishly on us that we are left speechless and deeply grateful for the work He has done in us as individuals and in our marriage.

Our hope and prayer is that you know He wants to do the same for you. God is for you and your marriage. He wants you to have a strong and safe friendship. God's heart longs for you to draw near to Him in difficult circumstances and to understand they don't have to pull you apart but, with His help, can give you the opportunity to grow closer together. His heart beats with excitement as you unite over your finances so you can fulfill your unique purpose as a couple by helping others. He wants nothing more than to be invited into your relationship so your intimacy is deepened not only physically but emotionally and spiritually as He alone is the One to meet our deepest needs. And He wants to surround you with others who can cheer you on in your journey. All of this is possible if you are intentional about making your wedding day vows an everyday reality. You got this! We are cheering for you!

For a downloadable version of

Our Intentional Check In, go to

www.kalamazoomarriageresource.com.

Our Intentional Check In

Rate how well you are doing together in each area.
1= not well to 5 = doing great!

PLAY____PRAY____PLAN____PURSUE GOD____PRESS ON____

Catching Up	1

- Our "win" for last week was_____
- Take turns completing the sentence "You did a great job____"
- Ask each other, "Do I owe you an apology for anything?

Our Vows	2

- When is our next date night?
- When can we pray together?
- Are we current with our budget?
- In what ways can we pursue God?
- Are our outside relationships helping or hurting our marriage?

Our Schedule	3

- Upcoming appointments:
- Upcoming events:
- What kind of self care do you need?

Around our house	4

- What chores need to be done?
- What big projects need completing?
- Who is going to do what?
- Is there a deadline?

Our Buckets	5

- What do you need physically?
- What do you need emotionally?
- What do you need spiritually?
- What do you need sexually?
- Other

Notes	6

The Vow we are focusing on this week

Our intentional action step is

One way I'm going to fill my spouse's bucket

One thing we are thankful for

Something we are looking forward to

About the Authors

Chad & Kristen Cottingham

Chad and Kristen have been married for thirty years. While their marriage began with a rocky start, their belief that marriage is God's design and the foundation of a healthy family were central to Chad and Kristen.

Their faith in Jesus and commitment to each other enabled them to overcome the challenges they faced through the years. Their passion to help strengthen marriages was birthed out of their own struggles and those close to them. By God's grace, they enjoy the privilege of teaching others what God has taught them!

Chad is a former teacher, school administrator and coach. Kristen is the author of *Life Beyond Laundry*, and is a women's motivational speaker and Bible teacher.

Together they service the directors of Kalamazoo Marriage Resource, where they write marriage building material, speak at events and share their experiences to help couples build their marriage.

Follow Kristen & Chad Cottingham on social media too!

 kalamazoomarriageresource.com

 Kalamazoo Marriage Resource

 @kalamazoomarriageresource

42676325R00173